W. B. Stewart

FRONTISPIECE TO HEAVEN'S ANTIDOTE.

"The chiming bells are calling upon all men to cut the cords of their earth-bound thoughts, and go up to worship at the footstool of Jehovah."—See p. 16.

PRIZE ESSAYS

ON

THE TEMPORAL ADVANTAGES

OF

THE SABBATH,

CONSIDERED IN RELATION TO THE WORKING CLASSES.

CONTAINING

HEAVEN'S ANTIDOTE, THE TORCH OF TIME, AND THE PEARL OF DAYS.

PHILADELPHIA:
PRESBYTERIAN BOARD OF PUBLICATION,
No. 265 CHESTNUT STREET.

Stereotyped by Wm. S. Slote, No. 19 St. James' Street,
Philadelphia.

PREFATORY NOTICE.

THE remarkable essays embodied in this volume were called forth by the offer of prizes for the three best essays on the temporal advantages of the Christian Sabbath to the labouring classes, by competitors from among the working men in Great Britain. Out of a large mass of manuscripts, three were selected by an impartial committee, and to the writers of them the prizes were adjudged. The first and third of these are here republished, and in place of the second, which is regarded as of inferior literary merit to the other two, another remarkable essay, entitled "The Pearl of Days," written by a female in humble life, has been substituted. As the productions of labouring *men* were exclusively contemplated in the offered prizes, this essay, admirable as it is in all respects, was not regarded by the committee as coming within the field of competition, but was highly applauded and recommended for separate publication for the author's benefit. The three essays, as here associated, will not be read merely as literary curiosities, proceeding as they do from persons of humble education and without any pretensions as professed authors, but will be esteemed for the solidity of their reasoning and for the impressive force with which they plead for a sacred observance of the Lord's day. They are as much needed in this country as in Great Britain, and the friends of religion and good order will hail their reproduction here at a time when the temptations to Sabbath desecration are so multiplied, and the moral sense of the community on the general subject is far from being in a healthy state.

For the appearance of this volume, and the handsome style in which it is published, the public is indebted to a generous individual who has made a special donation to the Presbyterian Board of Publication for this purpose, and who seeks occasions for manifesting his solicitude for the diffusion of those elevated moral principles which are at once the glory and safety of a nation.—Editor of the Board of Publication.

HEAVEN'S ANTIDOTE

TO THE

CURSE OF LABOUR;

OR

THE TEMPORAL ADVANTAGES OF THE SABBATH,

CONSIDERED IN RELATION TO THE WORKING CLASSES.

BY

JOHN ALLAN QUINTON, JOURNEYMAN PRINTER.

"Oh, day most calm, most bright,
The fruit of this, the next world's bud,
Th' indorsement of supreme delight,
Writ by a Friend, and with his blood;
The couch of time; care's balm and bay;
The week were dark but for thy light:
Thy torch doth show the way."

HERBERT.

CONTENTS.

ADJUDICATION NOTICE.

THE circumstances out of which this Essay originated were as follows:—Towards the close of the year 1847, a Christian gentleman, lamenting the fearful increase of Sabbath desecration by railway, steamboat, and other travelling facilities—deeply impressed with the intimate connection between the preservation of the Sabbath and national morality, prosperity, and order, and being convinced that many fallacies were propagated by those who, for their own profit, deprived the poor man of one of God's best gifts, the Sabbath, and then placed the responsibility of this robbery upon the poor man's shoulders, by declaring that they took the day from him for the benefit of himself or his fellow-workmen—determined to appeal to the working classes themselves, and obtain from them an unbiassed and impartial verdict upon this momentous subject. For this purpose he offered three prizes, of £25, £15, and £10, for the three best Essays upon "The Temporal Advantages of the Sabbath to the Labouring Classes, and the consequent importance of preserving its rest from all the encroachments of unnecessary labour." In the short space of about three months one thousand and forty-five Essays were received.

After a patient investigation of this vast mass of MSS., which occupied from the close of March to the close of December, 1848, we have awarded the three principal prizes as follows:—

First Prize, £25.—To John A. Quinton, Journeyman Printer, Ipswich.

Second Prize, £15.—To John Younger, Shoemaker, St. Boswell's Green, Roxburghshire.

Third Prize, £10.—To David Farquhar, Machinist, Dundee.

In making this award, we are constrained to throw ourselves upon the candid consideration of the competitors and the public. We have endeavoured to discharge our trust as in the sight of God, and we believe that we have selected the three best Essays. But we cannot court a rigid and formal criticism; nor dare we presume to anticipate that our judgment will be universally unimpeached. Those who are inclined to test its accuracy by some formal and preconceived model, will probably be disappointed with our decision, for the three principal Prizes are widely dissimilar in their structure, and may be said to represent three distinct orders of mind.

We feel these remarks the more necessary because it has been our privilege to obtain for the movement the patronage of Her Most Gracious Majesty the Queen, and His Royal Highness Prince Albert: His Royal Highness having contributed ten additional Prizes of £5 each, and the British public having already given upwards of seventy more. While these and other encouraging circumstances have greatly cheered us in our labour, they have drawn additional attention to our award, and rendered comparison and criticism much more easy and probable.

We cannot conclude this brief notice without expressing a hope that such further measures will be arranged as shall awaken an enlarged sympathy with the object throughout the British empire, and shall ensure the ultimate preservation of the entire of these valuable and interesting MSS.

ALEXANDER SWAN,
ROBERT KETTLE,
DANIEL FRANCIS OAKEY, } ADJUDICATORS.

London, Dec. 1848.

INTRODUCTION.

It had been the desire of those who are engaged in the direction of the Sabbath Essay movement, that the following Essay should have been introduced by one of the honorary editors, who is such a grace and ornament to the churches with which he is connected; and, but for the extreme pressure of his avocations, both in the pastorate and by the press, he would have complied with that desire. As it thus became necessary to seek some other for this office, I have gladly accepted the opportunity thereby afforded me, of evidencing my deep interest in this noble and gratifying labour of love amongst our hardworking brethren. Nor is this necessity without its advantages, since it gives occasion for exhibiting that evangelical unity amongst differing churches, which may be the harbinger of more peaceful and happy times, when Ephraim shall no longer envy Judah, nor Judah vex Ephraim, but Christian union shall be perfected, and made manifest in the whole body of Christ our Head. One of the Essayists, in reply to a letter I had occasion to address to him connected with a communication of his for the Working Man's Charter, observes, "May I be permitted to remark upon the singularity of my case, that the first approved literary effort of an humble member of a dissenting community should be ushered into the world under the auspices of a clergyman of the Church of England? May our united efforts in this labour of love receive the divine approbation." To this devout aspiration I heartily respond "Amen." May such interchanges of love and amity be more frequent. They are not altogether new. Dr. Doddridge, the Nonconformist minister, was the first editor of the pious and enlightened Archbishop Leighton's works, and a recent Bishop of Winchester, in his Elements of Theology, long a text-book for divinity students in our Universities, has placed in his list of elementary works the Commentary of Dr. Doddridge; while the simple and beautiful hymns of Dr. Watts are published under the sanction of the Christian Knowledge Society, and are as household words, as the very songs of Zion, in all families, and in all churches of the land. I cannot but rejoice, then, that it is permitted to me at once to take part in this most encouraging Sabbath movement, and at the same time to help on the great work of Christian union, by thus introducing to the notice of the religious world this deeply interesting and edifying composition, which is the work of one who is a member, and a valued and prized member, of the Independent Congregation of Ipswich, the town in which he has long been known, and which may well be proud of having thus been honoured by one of its working men.

The fact of our author being a working man, though undoubted amongst his own townsmen, is just that very one which it becomes us chiefly to certify our readers respecting. The Edinburgh Witness, a periodical of considerable influence and power, has not hesitated to say of this Essay, that it is one which any writer of any age might rejoice to have composed. And, as this is not only high, but deserved praise, it may excite doubts in the minds of some as to whether it really be the original and unaided production of the person it is represented as having been written by. It is not merely the public at large who are interested in this fact, as a remarkable literary incident; but all the fellow-competitors of our author are concerned to know that they have been dealt faithfully by in the adjudication, and that none but those justly entitled to a standing therein have been admitted to competition. But even more than all this, the holy and solemn cause itself in which these Essays have been written, demands imperatively of us that we substantiate the character and position of the writer, so as to prove beyond all dispute that he is of the class professed, and that, though in that class, he is capable of himself accomplishing the production of such a work as now appears from his hand, head, and heart.

We have felt bound, then, to seek the very best information upon this point, and we are happy to have it in our power to offer abundant testimony to the fact. The master in whose employment our author is, and has been for some years past, and who is himself well known in the town of Ipswich, has kindly favoured us with the following satisfactory reply to our request that he would furnish us with his testimonial.

Ipswich, Feb. 5, 1849.

DEAR SIR,

I have the pleasure of stating that Mr. Quinton has been twelve years in my establishment, that he has conducted himself in the most praiseworthy manner, and by his application and talent has gradually improved his position. He has been truly a working man, and all his distinctions are well earned.

I am, dear sir,

Yours faithfully,

To Rev. J. Jordan. J. M. BURTON.

As the foregoing is the testimony of his employer, the next shall be that of a personal friend, to whom our author referred us. He writes evidently with all the warmth of friendship, but at the same time with the earnestness of sincerity. In omitting, therefore, some passages of his letter, we can assure the reader that we do so mainly out of deference to an expression contained in a letter from Mr. Quinton himself, in which he writes, "I speak truly, when I say that I am very averse to this exposure before the public eye." We will not risk, then, the damage of such a feeling as this, while we must not shrink from discharging our duty to the public. Mr. Quinton's friend writes thus respecting him:

REV. SIR:

I cheerfully comply with your request in sending a few brief particulars respecting Mr. John Allan Quinton, whom I have known during nearly the whole time of my residence in Ipswich, a period of nine years, throughout which I have had opportunities of closely observing his conduct and deportment, and becoming acquainted with his position in life. He has been in Mr. Burton's employ during all that period, and is, strictly speaking, his servant. His employment is exclusively in the printing office, and he, in common with other working men, receives, as well as they, his weekly wages, although his length of service, ability, and conscientious, upright conduct have placed him in the position of foreman, or overseer.

His character, I believe, no one would attempt openly to impeach. Almost proverbial for integrity and uprightness; modest, diffident, unassuming; nature has done much for him; the grace of God has done more. He is greatly esteemed in the Christian community to which he belongs, and by his fellow-townsmen generally. . . . . His industry is highly commendable, and to this only can be attributed the attainments he has made in knowledge. His recreation is only a change of employment. . . . . Those who know most of him will speak in the highest terms of his character and industry. . . . .

What I have said I believe to be strictly in accordance with truth, and feel sure that my testimony would be confirmed by many to whom he is well known, and who have, like myself, cultivated his friendship.

I beg, sir, to subscribe myself,

Yours, most respectfully,

GEO. MESSENT.

Ipswich, Feb. 4, 1849.

The next testimony we would offer to the reader, is that of an intelligent member of the Society of Friends, resident at Ipswich, and for some time engaged in business as a banker—R. D. Alexander, Esq., F. L. S., whose frequent opportunities of knowing our author, and understanding his character and position, enable him to speak as satisfactorily as conclusively to these. Mr. Alexander writes thus:

Ipswich, 16; 2; 1849

RESPECTED FRIEND,

As one of John Allan Quinton's referees, I write to state that, in my character of editor of "The Temperance Recorder," and of a series of Temperance Tracts, I became acquainted with him about seven years since, when he was, and still continues to be, the foreman in Burton's printing office—hired by him as a "compositor," but of late years mostly, or almost entirely, occupied as overseer of the office, having from the increased work brought to the office —I have reason to believe in part from the good management of Quinton—little leisure to work at "the case." I have made very frequent, almost daily, visits to the printing office for a length of time, and have admired the quiet bearing of his manner, maintaining good order by gentle rule and respectful manner to those below him, aided by his unwearied industry and attention to his employer's work.

J. A. Quinton's conduct in private life is, I believe, consistent with his profession as a Christian, and in general terms I may say that he is a good example for working men.

I am respectfully,

RD. D. ALEXANDER.

We will present only one more testimonial, but it is that which, in every Christian community, is necessarily looked to as the most essential one—the good word of the minister of our holy faith under whose pastoral care Mr. Quinton lives, and whom, according to the ability given him, he aids in his work of inviting sinners to flee from the wrath to come, and to turn to repentance and calling upon God. The Rev. John Whitby, to whose kindness we are indebted for having communicated with the three gentlemen who have already borne their testimony to Mr. Quinton's worth, writes as follows:

Ipswich, Feb. 16, 1849.

REV. SIR,

I duly received yours, and saw Mr. Quinton on the subject, who, I believe, has written to you, and communicated the circumstantial facts you requested. I did not know him till he had ended his apprenticeship.

His membership with a Christian church began at Stowmarket. He has been some years in communion and membership with the church in Nicholas Chapel, of which I am the pastor. I had the pleasure of marrying him, some eight or nine years since, to one of our estimable members of the church.

He has always been a studious and persevering young man, with a comprehensive mind, and rather exuberant imagination. As a Christian, he has maintained a high and honourable reputation, much esteemed and beloved by true Christians. Nor has his Christian life been fruitless, but devoted to the cause of Christ. He has preached the Gospel, in villages and in my pulpit, with acceptance. I cherish a great regard for him, and so does the church of which he is a member. It is Christianity that has made him truly great. He has only written what he has enjoyed of the blessedness of keeping and loving the Sabbath. I was not surprised when I heard that he had reached the honour of the first prize on the Sabbath to the working classes. I knew his power of illustration. As to his eligibility as a working man to be a competitor, I may just say I have often seen him at work in the printing office of Mr. Burton, who, I believe, has written you in connection with the other gentlemen you mentioned. I need not add more.

I am, Rev. and dear sir,

Yours faithfully,

JOHN WHITBY,

Independent Minister.

Having now, as we trust, anticipated and satisfied every reasonable question that can be raised respecting our author, we are further desirous of gratifying what is likely to be the natural wish of every reader, and what has been the frequently expressed one of a large number of the competitors with whom we have had communication, that every Essayist should supply a brief account of himself, and thus make his fellow-competitors as well acquainted as possible with him, and the circumstances and occurrences of his life. Although, as stated above, our author would willingly, if consulting his own feelings alone, avoid such publicity, yet, for the sake of others, and especially for the sake of that cause in which he has been called upon to take so prominent a part, he consents to forego his own feelings, and has favoured us with a brief sketch of his life, which commences thus:

In the late honours that have been so unexpectedly thrust upon me, I have been unable to exercise any choice. I have been drawn, perforce, from the familiar sanctum of seclusion, and must cease more than ever to feel that I am *my own*, but am become more expressly the property of the Lord and his people. I will now proceed to register a few of the leading details of my past life, which has not been remarkable for any very striking incidents.

I was born at the small town of Needham Market, in the county of Suffolk, in the year 1817. I am the eldest of a family of either twelve or thirteen, ten of whom are living. My parents also are still living. I might observe, in passing, that they are respected for their unimpeachable lives and integrity of character. They have for many years been members of a Christian community. My father was a tailor by trade, but about thirty-six years ago he took a small chemist and druggist's shop, vacated by death, and by his uniform application to business and his eminent trustworthiness, he gradually extended and consolidated a snug little business, which has enabled him to bring up his large family in respectability and economic habits. At the age of nine or ten I was taken from a dame's school, and placed under the tutorage of Mr. J. Webb, then of Needham, but now Baptist Minister of Stoke Green Chapel, Ipswich. Mr. Webb, however, shortly after leaving to prosecute his college studies, I was transferred to the care of Mr. Durrant, with whom I continued till within a short period of my apprenticeship. This school was of the ordinary character to be found extensively, twenty years back, in villages and small towns. My education comprised writing, (anything but of a first-rate description,) arithmetic, reading, and grammar—and all these imparted in the most crude and meagre manner. If by education we are to understand the education of the mind, of this I had positively none. I was not conscious, for two or three years after completing my scholastic drudgeries, of any signs of intellectual life, or stirrings of mental wakefulness. Four or five years seem a long time to spend in amassing nothing, but a large portion of time was wasted in ornamental printing, &c., which was of no practical utility whatever. My instructor was a stenographer, and as I took a great deal of pleasure in the practice of this art, he was particularly gratified thereat, and gave me abundance of exercises and tasks, which, when performed, were rewarded with special marks of appreciation by a holiday. These things comprise the *tout ensemble* of my education. I never at school learned a sentence of geography, so far as I can recollect—no use of globes—no Latin—no study of maps—no drawing

—no history—no natural philosophy, &c. I never attempted a thesis or an essay, nor did I attempt such a task for years afterwards.

At the age of fourteen I was apprenticed to Mr. Woolby, printer and bookseller, Stowmarket, (three and a half miles from my native place,) with whom I continued six years. Being naturally indisposed to mix in society, I kept myself quite retired, seldom going out after or before business hours, even for requisite exercise. This confinement, chiefly self-imposed, and this consequent deficiency of physical recreation, superinduced a feebleness of constitution that has unfitted me for years for any severe or prolonged muscular exertion. The first two or three years of my apprenticeship were devoted to the study of music, the reading of poetry, sometimes novels, and works of general information. I soon evinced a taste for works of an imaginative and exciting character, and for a poetical style of composition. Of some of Byron's works I was passionately fond. From reading, I soon began to write, poetry. I lived in a land of dreams and ideal enchantments. The poetic afflatus or inspiration has oftentimes emasculated my strength, filled me with trembling, and compelled me to desist from labour. I grew disgusted with the mean and gross realities of common life. I felt inarticulate longings for something above the actual. This state of feeling and emotion breathed itself out in innumerable fragmentary effusions. About this time I became a Sabbath School teacher, and shortly after, through instrumentality in connection with the school, I was brought to decision of character. For a long period of years I never remember to have absented myself from a place of worship, which I almost invariably attended three times on the Sabbath. Coeval with these circumstances, I might mention, a society for Mutual Improvement was established, directed, and presided over, by gentlemen of considerable mental culture and attainments. This institution

I joined, and here my first decided public efforts were made to emancipate my mind from the thraldom of ignorance.

On April 1st, 1836, I was received into fellowship with the Independent Church, Stowmarket, then under the pastoral care of Rev. W. Ward, M. A. (since deceased). My attention was now almost entirely absorbed by religious reading, exercises, and correspondence, and by visiting the sick and ignorant. I also had earnest desires stirred up in my mind towards the ministry of the Gospel. On the expiration of my term of apprenticeship, having in purpose renounced my secular calling, and being in a precarious state of health, I returned home with the intention of recruiting the same, and waiting the developments of God's will in this matter. Here I continued for about eight months, employed in reading, and occasional preaching in the surrounding villages. I likewise undertook the superintendence of a Sabbath school. As winter drew on, however, and no means wherewith to prosecute my introductory studies, previous to a collegiate course, were apparent, I began to grow uncomfortable in burdening my parents, and thought I had mistaken the path of duty. I accordingly, in the month of December, came to Ipswich in order to obtain a situation. I was, by a singular concurrence of circumstances, directed to Mr. Burton's—engaged with him—where I have continued ever since. His business was then very small, but from that period until now (more than twelve years) it has steadily increased in every department. He has now machines worked by steam power, a stereotype foundry, &c., and every facility for doing work in the best style. My province has been exclusively in the office, and, to a considerable extent, the management of the printing office has been entrusted to me. During all this long period I have closely applied myself to business through long hours, but as I did it cheerfully, and with an indomitable determination to battle upwards, its oppressiveness was not so painfully felt. My leisure for reading and intellectual culture has accordingly been exceedingly limited. I believe I should be within the mark if I said that, on an average, I have not read twenty volumes, small and large, light and solid, per year. I begin to feel this deprivation now very keenly, and long for more literary and religious leisure. Until within the last two years I have regularly engaged in the villages as an evangelist. Enfeebled health now forbids such exhausting labours.

Such, dear sir, is a plain unvarnished statement of the leading events of my unexciting history. I leave them in your judicious hands, to make what use of them you may deem proper. But the less parade the better, if my feelings are to be consulted. I shall be happy to answer any question which may be suggested by the foregoing facts.

Such is our friend's unvarnished tale of himself and his earlier years. In concluding this introduction we will add a brief remark respecting the Essay itself, and the position assigned to it. It is not detracting from the merits of either this, the first, or the other two, the second and third Essays, selected out of so large a number as one thousand and forty-five competitors, to say, that they have not attained to their honourable position without much anxious discrimination on the part of those who adjudicated respecting them. So far is this from being the case, that we hail it rather as a testimony of the anxiety and faithfulness with which the adjudication was carried on, as an omen for good respecting the whole movement, and as a corroborative assurance that, while there were others esteemed worthy to compete closely with these for the superiority, there are special and pecu liar excellencies in the three which entitle them to their place and reward.

The one immediately before us will not fail, we are persuaded, to commend itself to the reader, for its evident and obvious appropriateness to the solemn subject discussed in it, under the peculiar phase demanded by the terms of the competition. There may be others of apparently more vivacity and power—others, again, that seem to manifest closer and severer judgment—others still, irradiating sparks of apparently more fervid and devout piety; but for a noble combination of all these, developed with a staidness and sobriety of thought adapted to the subject, and enlivened with rich and eloquent strains of exhortation, we believe that no other will be found to rival it, and that it will thus abundantly justify the final decision respecting it, and approve itself to all as thus rightly placed, whatever comparisons may be hereafter instituted between it and others, as they severally appear, and as, no doubt, their respective friends and admirers may be tempted to urge in their behalf.

It is, then, with entire confidence that we commend both the work and its author to the favour and interest of all who would cherish in their hearts a due reverence for God's holy day, and that affection and love for the class of persons from whom this Essay emanates, which those cannot fail to have who understand and appreciate the apostolical injunction, "As we have many members in one body, and all members have not the same office, so we, being many, are one body in Christ, and every one members one of another." Rom. xii. 4, 6.

J. JORDAN.

Enstone, Oxon, Feb. 1849.

HEAVEN'S ANTIDOTE TO THE CURSE OF LABOUR.

WE are entering on what may be emphatically styled the Age of Progress. But our advancement does not consist, in all cases, in pursuing with accelerated speed the track trodden by our progenitors. These are rather times of sifting investigation. Everything is being tested. Every received dogma is submitted to the crucible. Every object of popular faith and homage is subjected to the most keen and rigid scrutiny. Every social and religious institution has passed, or is passing, the same fiery ordeal. Men are digging down to discover the deep foundations of things.

A stern spirit of utilitarianism is abroad, plucking up whatsoever is useless, and overthrowing whatsoever is obstructive of the prosperity and progression of man. Some of the most sacred objects commanding our love and veneration, as well as many of the imposing shams that have fed and thriven on popular credulity, have been, from time to time, assailed and denounced by their adversaries. The Bible has been again and again cast into the furnace of controversy, but always to come out more glorious and precious than before. Christianity, too, has often engaged in desperate conflict with her embattled foes, but has always retained possession of the field, and come off more than conqueror. On the other hand, numerous systems of error, excrescences of ancient institutions, and creations of human selfishness, that once flourished in the world, have shrivelled beneath the exposures of the intelligent and the good. At the present period, many of these lately reigning pretences, impeached by reason and condemned by public opinion, are slowly perishing from our midst.

We need not be surprised, therefore, that the SABBATH—an institution crossing fallen man's self-interest at such a variety of points, and tolerant of none of the grosser or more grovelling predilections of the masses—should come in for its full share of hostility and repudiation. Avarice grudges it, and would be glad to buy it up. Selfishness covets it, and waits only for a plausible pretext to seize upon and annex it to its domains. Sensuality gloats upon it, and, scorning its alleged sanctity, would spend it in a carnival of folly and voluptuousness. Infidelity would raise its shouts of triumph on beholding it trampled down by worldliness, whilst religious lukewarmness holds its entreasured blessings with such a relaxing grasp, that it would not require a very powerful effort to wrench them from its custody. But the Sabbath has most to fear from the gigantic public companies everywhere springing up around us in this age of enterprise. What isolated individuals would shrink from the responsibility of attempting, confederacies, strong in wealth and in influence, will be found daring enough to do, and that, too, with comparative impunity. Many of these leagues of selfishness, we fear—whose greed is concentrated and intensified by their numbers—would not scruple to stretch forth their monopolizing hands and appropriate this day to schemes of aggrandizement. But, should they ever be suffered to extort this blessing from society, and silence all indignant remonstrance, no earthly power would be able to stand against their desolating inroads. The health, the domestic comfort, the moral elevation, and the spiritual welfare of the labouring classes, would be of no more account than the small dust of the balance. The happiness of thousands of lowly families would be speedily and remorselessly sacrificed. Multitudes of human beings, dear to their kindred, dear to their country, and dear to their Creator and Redeemer, would thus become the mere "tools of gain—the conscripts of ambition—and the materials of luxury."

If such a catastrophe is to be averted, the friends of humanity and the guardians of truth must awake from their lethargy, and bravely go forth to repulse the invaders of the Sabbath. Should the Sabbath's privileges be wrested from the sons of toil, it can only happen through the apathy and the unfaithfulness of the philanthropic and the good. But if every one who is baptized with love for his species would diligently study the subject in all its bearings, master its apparent difficulties, get distinct views of it before his own mind, and then do his utmost towards the creation of a healthy public opinion on the matter, the ominous evils now menacing our country would be immediately checked—the designs of the sordid, the profane, and the licentious would be frustrated—the claims of the Sabbath would be established on an immovable basis—the tide of Sabbath desecration would be rolled back, and a glorious impetus would be given to the holy enterprises of the age.

Should the following investigation of the temporal advantages of the Sabbath, considered especially in relation to the working classes, tend, however feebly, to aid a "consummation so devoutly to be wished," the writer will have accomplished an object lying very near to his heart.

The plan we propose to pursue will be, to commence with the subordinate benefits conferred by the Sabbath, and gradually ascend to the contemplation of those affecting the higher interests of mankind. And should we be tempted to dwell longer on these inferior advantages than may be thought necessary, it will be in consequence of their being usually very inadequately set forth, and because they are actually realized by far greater numbers than are those of a more exalted character. We shall notice—

I. THE PHYSICAL ADVANTAGES OF THE SABBATH.

Among these may be enumerated repose, cleanliness, and health.

I. REPOSE.

Man needs periodic intervals of rest. The strongest constitutional stamina, the most robust or sinewy human frame, must speedily relax beneath the exactions of the mildest forms of continuous labour. A kind provision is partially made to avert this result, by the season of nocturnal repose, when the benevolent Creator, quenching the glare of day, and drawing the curtains of darkness around a wearied world, enfolds the children of creation beneath the shadow of his wings, and hushes them to slumber on their beds of peace. But this sweet restorative—welcome as it always is to human infirmity, and anxiously as it is longed for, as the day drags to its close, by multitudes overmastered by the severities of toil and the monotonous struggles of life—does not fully meet the exigencies of man's nature. The nightly supply of refreshment and strength is not equivalent to the daily expenditure of energy ordinarily incurred; and especially is this true in vast numbers of cases among the working classes, where the constitution has been deteriorated by early privations, by insufficiency of food, and by uncleanly or intemperate habits. A supplemental period of rest is therefore required, to treasure up such a degree of strength as shall enable those upon whom the burden of labour presses most heavily, to fulfil their allotted tasks without prematurely wearing out the animal system.

But neither is this all. It is not enough that a race of rational beings should be dealt with on the mercenary principles adopted with respect to our beasts of burthen. Man's two-fold nature—his nobler capabilities—his elevation as a moral agent—his soul, resplendent even in its ruins—challenge a loftier recognition of his claims than is due to the mere drudges of creation. To calculate the daily ravages committed upon the loins, the muscles, and the limbs of labour, and to dole out the minimum amount of rest and nutriment that will suffice to repair these damages—to barely maintain the equilibrium of functional waste and supply, at the smallest possible sacrifice of their services—is to embrute the labouring population; yea, to degrade beings originally fashioned in the image of God into mere animate machines, to be used in the production of wealth, luxury, and patrician indulgences, in which they are never suffered to participate; instead of which, they are doomed—through the elasticity of youth, the vigour of manhood, and the decrepitude of age—to spend all their intervals of relaxation from physical exertion in eating, in drinking, or in sleeping—and all this only to gather fresh power for the strained sinews, and new moisture for the dripping brow! But man yearns for a higher order of repose than this: something more congenial with the diviner indwellings of his being. Not the mere oblivion of the senses; not the luxurious stretch of the tired limbs; not the subdued throbbings of the overwrought brain; not alone the casting out of mortal weariness and pain;—not a rest altogether imposed by physical necessity, but a rest that may be wakefully, intelligently, and complacently enjoyed. Such a want is delightfully supplied by the institution of the Sabbath!

The wisdom as well as the benevolence of Heaven is clearly exemplified in this ordinance, in its manifest adaptation to the circumstances of the bulk of mankind. These days are not "like angels' visits, few and far between;" nor is the respite from secular employment, when it arrives, too protracted in its duration. It preserves a judicious mean between these mischievous extremes. Had its recurrence fallen at intervals more distant than at present, its benign influence would have been found insufficient to withstand the crushing effects of unremitting labour on the health of our operatives. And, on the other hand, if it had occurred oftener, it would have exposed multitudes to privations, from the scantiness of their earnings; it might have tended to undermine those industrial habits upon which the working classes have to rely for their prosperity and advancement; and might, moreover, have increased those propensities to indolence and dissipation, which even now are too extensively disclosed. As it is, the Sabbatical rest, whilst it affords but a brief holiday to idleness, suffices to oil the wheels of industry, to give new zest to enterprise, and to renerve the arm, and gird up afresh the loins of labour.

The Sabbath, as a day of relaxation and refreshment, should be esteemed precious by the working classes in particular. The statesman, the merchant, the manufacturer, and even the tradesman, can often escape the duties or emancipate themselves from the thrall of business; and, vanishing from their respective engagements, may embark for foreign travel, and luxuriate awhile in some invigorating clime; or, wandering up and down our own fair isle in search of health, may halt at spots rich in historic interest and in memorials of ancient fame, or may visit the wonder-teeming cities and towns reared by modern enterprise; or else, if wearied with the excitement of such scenes, may turn aside for a season to the margin of the ocean, and there inhale health and gladness from its bracing breezes, refresh their bodies in its living waters, and soothe the irritation of their feelings with the music of its murmurings. But not so the poor working man; he cannot go beyond his tether—he can rarely cast off his collar. From morning's dawn to evening's close, and often into the deep shadows of the night—through scenes of sorrow and tribulation, and the incipient stages of disease—his necessities chain him to his post. Condemned, like Sisyphus of old, to roll the stone of labour up the steep acclivity of life, which, on having neared the summit, rebounds to its starting point again, he finds himself, after the disbursement of his scanty wages, again at the bottom of the mountain, yoked to his hopeless task, and compelled to begin anew the up-hill struggle.

But cheer thee, child of travail! The blessed Sabbath is thine own! It is the excellent gift of thy Maker—see, then, that no man rob thee of the boon! It is the heir-loom of thy family—see that it be not alienated from their possession! It is a sacred inheritance, bequeathed by successive generations of the godly—see, then, that its frail fences are kept unbroken, and that its fruitful soil is not, through neglect, cursed with sterility and nakedness! The fifty-two Sabbaths of rest with which the year is interspersed are like patches of verdure, watered by ever-springing fountains, that dot the inhospitable wilderness, and invite its fainting travellers to exhilaration and repose. They are the ports that fringe the sea of human industry, in which the distressed bark may find a sure anchorage, and where it may renew its outfit for time and for eternity.

Oh, precious day! the workman's jubilee—the slave's release—the shield of servitude—the antidote of weariness—the suspension of the curse! How it smoothes the brow of care! How it brightens the countenance of gloom! How it braces the enervated limbs of labour! How it revives the drooping spirit of despair! How it gives wings to the clogged affections and aspirations of the soul! How it pours some drops of sweetness on the bitterest lot, and sheds some gleams of sunshine athwart the saddest heart! How it lifts the groveller from his low pursuits, and fills him with a noble self-respect! How it extinguishes the jealousies and rivalries of week-day occupations, and links men's hearts in the bonds of brotherhood! It does homage to the glorious attributes of the man, even when it finds him in the condition of the serf. In most cases it proclaims to the servant equal liberty with the master. It is a perpetual rebuke to the reigning rapacity of the world. It deals out, with even-handed justice, the essential rights of manhood, to all classes alike; and is designed to protect the poor from the bribes of wealth, and the weak from the encroachments of power.

Companions in labour! have you never attempted to compute the value of the Sabbath, even in this, the meanest of its uses, as a provision of rest for the body? Have any among you been wont scornfully to repudiate it, as an institution originated and upheld by the craft of priests? Do you regard its weekly advent as an unwelcome intrusion—as a perpetual restriction on your privileges, a curb to your enterprise, and a sacrifice to your pocket? Can you read no inscription of Divine loving-kindness on its serene brow, and discover none of the gifts strewn by its bountiful hands? Are you accustomed to yawn away its lagging hours in idleness, or sport them away in folly or in wantonness? Oppressed by the insipidity of inaction, do you cry, "Oh, what a weariness it is! When will the Sabbath be gone, that we may sell corn, and set forth the refuse of the wheat?—that we may dress the vineyard, plough the field, weld the metal, print the book, weave the cloth, make the garment, build the house, or garnish the sepulchre?" Brethren! reflect seriously on these things; and though it should appear that the Sabbath was ordained for no higher purpose than to minister to the animal refreshment of man, yet even this is a blessing of such priceless worth, that to wring it from the possession of society would superinduce a catastrophe too frightful to contemplate.

That the Sabbath is no modern ecclesiastic innovation, and that it is not an exploded ordinance of the Jewish economy engrafted upon the Christian system, are clear from acknowledged records of a remote antiquity; some of which furnish indubitable proofs of a general tradition respecting the primitive Sabbath. Hesiod, who lived about 900 years before the advent of Christ, says, "The seventh day is holy." Homer, who sang about the same period, and Callimachus, likewise a Greek poet, who flourished about 700 years later, allude to the seventh day as holy. Theophilus, of Antioch, says, concerning the seventh day, "The day which all mankind celebrate." Porphyry says, "The Phœnicians consecrated one day in seven as holy." Lucian remarks, "The seventh day is given to school-boys as a holiday." Eusebius observes, "Almost all the philosophers and poets acknowledge the seventh day as holy." Clemens Alexandrinus says, "The Greeks, as well as the Hebrews, observe the seventh day as holy." Josephus, the Jewish historian, says, "No city of Greeks or barbarians can be found which does not acknowledge a seventh day's rest from labour." Philo testifies, "The seventh day is a festival to every nation." Thus, through a long succession of ages, and by numerous Gentile nations, who were not at all likely to adopt any one of the exclusive rites of Judaism, we have ample evidence that the seventh day has been observed, with more or less of religious ceremonial, as a period of relaxation for the wearied body, and as a temporary asylum from the wasting strifes and cares of life. The illustrations furnished above point unquestionably to vestiges of the primeval Sabbath, instituted in Paradise, and which had been republished to the new world by Noah and his posterity—memorials of which were thus preserved among heathen races, despite the prevalence of depravity and the growth of human selfishness, not so much from veneration for the high authority that prescribed it, as from an appreciation of its suitableness and profitableness for the burdened masses of mankind.

A really sanctified Sabbath throughout the world would exhibit impressive proofs of the Divine benignity, and would present to the devout mind, even in its merely picturesque aspects, one of the most interesting spectacles that could be witnessed upon earth. Go forth at early morning, and climb the side of an upland peak, contiguous to some thickly-peopled city. Gaze eastward, southward, westward, and northward—through the whole circuit travelled by the sun—and behold the delectable representation of Sabbath rest. Every sound breathes softer; every tint gleams brighter; every scene seems fresher. Cast thy glance across the country—pass from field to field, from rill to river, from alp to glen, from hill to valley, from grove to grove, from one cluster of human dwellings to another, and read in every softened feature of nature the sweet tranquillity of Sabbath rest!

The flocks are wandering and gambolling in the dells; the cattle are grazing on the hill-sides; and the beasts of burden, freed from their yoke, are feeding on the open plains. The plough stands where it halted in its course across the furrows; but the husbandman is gone home to cultivate his soul. The sound of the axe has ceased from the forest, and the prostrate trees lie as they fell; but the woodman is gone away to ponder on the sudden death-stroke that may lay him low, or is on his way to the place where the keen axe of truth will be levelled at the roots of his stubborn sins. The mills are at rest on every hill-top, but their inmates have retired to their habitations to garner up the corn of heaven. Few men are seen abroad; they are chiefly at home, by the domestic hearth, beside the family altar, teaching groups of children, watching at the couch of sickness, or smoothing the pillow, and pouring balmy speech into the ear of the dying. Again behold and rejoice over the glorious benefits of Sabbath rest!

Turn next towards the great city, rearing its roofs, chimneys, steeples, monuments, and huge masses of masonry in an atmosphere less murky and impure than that which broods over it on the other days of the week. The swarms of industry are now hived. The mingled hum of busy multitudes, the heavy tramp of traffic, the rush of enterprise, the clamour of human passions, the noise of innumerable tools and implements of handicraft, the fierce panting of engines, the ringing of anvils, and the furious racings of machinery; the shouts of crowds, the brawls of drunkenness, and the plaints of mendicant misery, are all sunk into silence, and disturb not with a ripple of agitation the still Sabbath air. The huge factories and workshops that girdle the city, and which are the fountains of its prosperity, are empty and dumb; and the swarms that carry on their earthly burrowings in those warrens of industry are reposing themselves in the companionship of their families. The tall ships at anchor in the harbour have furled their sails, closed down their hatches, and hid from all eyes the merchandise treasured in their holds, whilst the Bethel-flag waves amidst a forest of masts, and they that go down to the sea, and do business on great waters, are below, studying the chart of Revelation, tracing the dangers of their life's voyage, and anticipating the glad hour when, redeemed from every peril, and borne on the bosom of a favouring tide, they shall safely moor their bark in the haven of eternal life. The black and dusty wharves, usually the Babel-scenes of confusion, are cleared of their hordes of porters, and clerks, and captains, and loitering crews, who have cast off their burdens along with their foul skins and rough garments, and are now lading themselves with the rich freightage of the Holy Word. The merchant has quitted the desk of his dusky counting-house, and is now, in secret places, turning over the blotted leaves of his own heart. The shopman has left his counter, the weaver his loom, the joiner his bench, the smith his forge, and the broker his stall, for the new Sabbath, in its advent, has published to all its tidings of liberty and rest.

The gates of the temple of Mammon are shut, and the gods of gold and silver are forsaken by their week-day devotees. The chiming bells, sounding alike across country and town, are calling upon all men to cut the cords of their earth-bound thoughts and low cares, and go up to worship at the footstool of Jehovah; and the tapering spires, like holy fingers, are pointing significantly towards the sky

And now the minister is descending from his study, his countenance impressed with a solemn sense of his responsibility; the saint is coming forth refreshed from his closet; the pardoned penitent is rising from his knees; the evangelist is on his way to his mission work; the Sabbath-school teacher is pleading with his class, and the Christian matron is gently leading forth her children to the mountain of the Lord's house.

At length a new traffic fills the streets; a growing bustle stirs the air; a new scene expands before the eye. Religious assemblies are gathering the major part of the population. They come from the spacious squares and the crowded lanes; they are seen issuing alike from the lordly palace and the plebeian hut. Trooping together are seen gray-haired sires and sprightly youth; the widow in her weeds and the virgin in her teens; the father in hale manhood and the mother in her charms; the lofty in their grandeur and the lowly in their simplicity; the mighty in their pride and the feeble in their meekness; the healthy in their bloom and the sickly in their paleness; the saint with his pleasant gravity and the sinner with his indifference; the coxcomb in his daintiness and the rustic in his rudeness. They pass along, not with the swift-footedness of week-day enterprise, but with a measured step and gait, befitting the solemn associations of the day. Gradually their numbers are diminished, and ere long the throng has disappeared, whilst the silence of the streets is broken only by the footfall of some lonely passenger. They are gone to the places where the rich and poor meet together on terms of equality—where world-made distinctions are effaced—and where one common Father looks down, with impartial benignity and grace, on priest and people, on peer and pauper, on sovereign and slave. The bells grow dumb one by one, and the doors of the sanctuaries shut in their congregated worshippers.

Organs are pealing through the lofty roofs of cathedrals, and along the aisles of churches; anthems are swelling from scores of unseen chapels; the glad outbursts of thanksgiving and the hallelujahs of the happy are mingling in the air, and filling the clear vault of heaven with rich harmony. Then the holy breath of prayer goes up like fragrant incense, ascending to the sky; after which the manna of the word is scattered round the camp, and the doctrines of grace are distilled like reviving dew upon the parched hearts of men. Prayer and praise again succeed, and then—convinced by some eloquent Apollos, or conscience-stricken by some vehement Paul, or comforted by some consoling Barnabas, or melted by some fervent John—the assemblies break up and return, fervently ejaculating their gratitude for the priceless privileges of Sabbath rest!

Alas! that the preceding sketch of Sabbath sanctification should seem so much like an ideal creation. Its observance, in the most favoured spots of our world, is but a remote approximation to its destined quietude and purity. The picture is everywhere blotted and blurred. Clouds of human depravity darken its divine beauty. The greed of covetousness has wrung from its hands some of its noblest blessings, while the natural impiety of man's heart, and the constraints of his evil habits, complete the awful work of desecration. God has given the day, and blind selfishness not only wrongs itself of the invaluable boon, but would lay an embargo upon its free blessings in relation to others also. Sloth is seen foolishly idling away the golden hours. Profaneness is heard uttering its coarse jests and blasphemies in the very precincts of the sanctuary. Profligacy comes forth meretriciously attired, and, heedless of rebuke, tracks the very footsteps of the pious. The "lovers of pleasure," transported by the wild liberty of the day, rush into scenes of sinful excitement—crowd the steamboats, riot in suburban tea-gardens, or promenade the streets, the parks, or the river's banks. Trains rush across the startled country, robbing thousands of railway servants of their heritage of rest, and pouring influxes of dissipated strangers into quiet villages and distant towns, whence, after roaming and carousing for hours, they are again borne back by the returning train, but not without having given an additional stimulus to all that was evil, and leaving behind them broad sowings of demoralization, destined to spring up and yield a wild produce of corruption and sorrow in future years.

II. CLEANLINESS.

The Sabbath is productive of habits of cleanliness. Superficial thinkers might, possibly, pronounce this alleged advantage to be foreign and far-fetched; but a dip beneath the surface will reveal its intimate relation to the day, and invest it with an importance that cannot well be exaggerated. Recent investigations have brought to light a revolting picture of squalor, impurity, and wretchedness, herding together in the crowded avenues and courts of our great towns and cities. Philanthropy has pleaded earnestly and long for the removal of these nests of social abomination, and the public, catching at length the same humane inspiration, are sternly demanding that sweeping sanatory measures should be adopted to get rid of these receptacles of corruption and nurseries of crime. Now, to the outcasts self-banished to these regions, the Sabbath never comes! In vain its morning eye peeps kindly in at the patched and gloomy windows, for it meeteth no recognition there! In vain its meridian beams, struggling through the murkiness and filth above, around, beneath, seek to shine into the doorways of those den-like homes, for they are quickly quenched by the deep darkness that abideth there! There the Sabbath's decencies are never cultivated, the Sabbath's peace is never enjoyed, the Sabbath's festival is never kept, the Sabbath's blessing is never known!

But oh! what augmented numbers of the working classes would become the irredeemable victims of this dark lot if the Sabbath were repealed! The periodical return of the Sabbath supplies a powerful motive to the cultivation of the proprieties of life. It promotes, at regularly recurring intervals, the purification of the dwelling, the cleansing of household utensils, and the lustration and anointing of the person. By what washings and purgings, by what scourings and polishings, by what decorations and trimmings is its near approach announced! What multitudes of buckets, and brushes, and dust disturbers are called into active requisition, and what streams of beautiful water are spoiled to remove the unclean accumulations of the week, and to offer a fitting tribute to the purity of the day. The greasy coating of mingled dirt and perspiration, deposited day by day upon the surface of the body, is cast off with the soiled work-day dress, and those whose calling brings them continually into defiling contacts are permitted to know the deliciousness and delight of a purified skin.

And then, when the day of hebdomadal release arrives, and, denuded of every badge of servitude, and appareled in his best garments, the transformed artisan steps forth from his abode into the presence of others metamorphosed like himself, what manly and dignified feelings are awakened in his breast; and, on finding himself saluted by his superiors in station, what feelings of self-respect will arise in his soul! Thus the Sabbath counteracts the inevitable tendency of the servilities of labour—it is perpetually at war with the sad effects of the curse, for, whilst menial occupations gradually undermine and lower a man in his own estimation, and shroud the excellence of his being in mysterious darkness, it is the aim of the Sabbath, by the hallowing associations into which it ushers him, to impress him with a sense of the solemnity of his position and the grandeur of his destiny.

It is impossible to overrate the beneficial influence of the habits of cleanliness thus superinduced, upon the health, decencies, and morals of the labouring population. It is an influence so constant in its operation, and so comprehensive in its range, that none but the most abandoned in character and condition can resist its assimilating action, and these escape it only by fleeing to some dark retreat on the first approach of the Sabbath's sun, where they will hide their shame and filthiness till the Monday's bustle again calls them forth, to prowl up and down and prey upon the world. Besides, this luxury of purification and this beauty of order, enjoyed by the provident and thrifty on the Sabbath, by no means terminate with the close of that day, but, following them through the week, and through the year, and through the successive stages of life, materially aid in the formation of the general character of that great class among the people. For those who are accustomed to study the phenomena of society will find it to be an almost invariable law, that improvidence and impurity go hand in hand—that profligacy and physical filthiness are twin evils, whilst devotion ever companies with decency, and piety has always a fitting symbol of itself in external cleanliness.

Thus one benefit comes not alone. Cleanliness allures and leads the way to other graces. Physical benefits are often a prelude to moral blessings. The appendages of the body become a true index to the condition of the mind. The dwelling, like a faithful mirror, reflects from every side an image of the family, and household life, in its revolving phases, is but the visible development of the habits and garniture of the soul.

The objection may be started to the foregoing lines of argumentation, that if the Sabbath's visitation did not present its appeals to the cleanly propensities of the people, other opportunities would be sought and set apart by them for the realization of so desirable an object as that at which we have glanced.

But when, we seriously ask, are such opportunities, recurring with sufficient frequency, to be found? When would there occur such a confluence of powerful motives, favoured by adequate leisure, as would stimulate, not here and there an isolated individual or a solitary family only, but large masses of the working classes, to the cultivation of the proprieties and amenities of life? Where, amid the fierce contentions, the grinding extortions, the lustful rivalries, and the everlasting labours of a Sabbathless world, would these blessed pauses be met with? Nay, the spirit of the mechanic would be so paralysed and abased as to make him utterly reckless of all decent appearances. Every finer instinct and every germ of greatness would perish in his nature; and these gone, and together with them every facility and incentive to self-improvement, the man would degenerate into the brute, and communities of such beings would become awful scourges in the earth. We solemnly believe that the Sabbath alone, by its universal provisions, its benignant restraints, and its proclamations of mercy, stands angel-like between us and this abyss of ruin.

III. HEALTH.

The Sabbath is eminently conducive to health. Health consists in the proper performance of the functions of those organs which constitute the body of man: it is the perfection of the physical system. The preservation of health depends upon the maintenance of the energy of the living functions, which, when severely tasked by protracted labour, can only be restored by commensurate repose and recreation, and by such other exercises as tend to impart vivacity and exhilaration to the mind. Now, these indispensable advantages, as we have attempted to show, are guaranteed by the Sabbath, and that in far more abundance and with greater certainty than could be otherwise secured.

The weekly Sabbath comes to sprinkle its reviving dews on the hot brow of industry, and administer the elixir of life to a fainting world.

A moderate amount of physical effort, proportioned to the degree of muscular energy possessed, and interspersed by intervals of refreshment, contributes decidedly to the development of the strength and well-being of the frame; but wherever the tasks of toil are pitilessly multiplied—where the shoulders can never throw off the yoke—where the spur is ceaselessly applied to the poor fettered slave—such a course of stimulation must strain and derange the delicate mechanism, engender disease and premature decay, and goad the body, with unnatural swiftness, into the bosom of a welcome grave.

Health is unquestionably the greatest temporal blessing sweetening the condition of those who are dependent for their subsistence on manual labour. It is the chief element in the scanty capital of the poor operative. Rob him of this, and you reduce him to pauperism and want. While health tints his countenance, nerves his arm, wings his feet, exhilarates his spirits, and pours a spring-tide of energy through the channels of life, the robust mechanic will sport with labour, laugh at poverty, and find existence to be a luxury and a joy. But, when the health sickens and the strength declines—when the arm hangs pithless and the eye grows dull—then it is that confidence reels, the buoyant spirits droop, and hope—that heavenly guest, which is the first to come and the last to leave the human bosom—languishes and dies. It is a sorrowful sight to behold the delicate and sickly compelled by dire necessity to bend their weakness to efforts suited only to the athletic—to see the shriveled limb straining its feebleness to earn some scanty pittance, and the decrepid form borne to the dust in painfulness beneath its cruel load. Yet such sights are at present mournfully common in our world. We cannot walk along our streets, or visit the retreats of industry and the marts of business, without having our eyes grieved and our hearts pained by their recurrence.

But if man fade so rapidly, with a seventh portion of his time consecrated to rest and renovation, then what imagination can conceive the frightful condition into which he would be plunged if the barriers of the Sabbath were hurled down, and reclining humanity were summoned from its repose to commence a life of uninterrupted bondage! If the wear and tear of the beautiful machine be attended with so much mischief now, how fearful would be the destruction of health and life under a system so grinding and ruthless! How dreary and death-like would the world become! Its workshops would resemble the wards of some mighty hospital, tenanted by the pining victims of intense toil. Manhood would, in one or two generations, lose all its characteristic strength; youth would be smitten with a fatal blight ere it had half attained its growth, and hale old age would soon become a prodigy to be wondered at in the land.

Yokefellows! think how the abstraction of the Sabbath would hopelessly enslave the working classes, with whom we are identified. Think of labour thus going on in one monotonous and eternal cycle—the limbs for ever on the rack, the fingers for ever plying, the eye-balls for ever straining, the brow for ever sweating, the feet for ever plodding, the brain for ever throbbing, the shoulders for ever drooping, the loins for ever aching, and the restless mind for ever scheming. Think—as your imagination beholds the unvarying wheel of work, the tread-mill of labour, thus going round, and round, and round, without a change, without a pause, from morn to night, from moon to moon, and from year to year—think, if you can, of the desolations that must follow this absolute reign of labour over the whole realm of time. Think of the beauty it would efface; of the merry-heartedness it would extinguish; of the giant strengths that it would tame; of the resources of nature that it would exhaust; of the aspirations it would crush; of the sicknesses that it would breed; of the projects it would wreck; of the groans that it would extort; of the lives that it would immolate; and of the cheerless graves that it would prematurely dig! See them, toiling and moiling, sweating and fretting, grinding and hewing, weaving and spinning, strewing and gathering, sowing and reaping, razing and building, digging and planting, unlading and storing, striving and struggling;—in the garden and in the field, in the granary and in the barn, in the factory and in the mill, in the warehouse and in the shop, on the mountain and in the ditch, on the road-side and in the wood, in the city and in the country, on the sea and on the shore, on the earth and in the earth, in days of brightness and days of gloom, in hours of sun and seasons of storm, in times of trouble and times of peace, in the heights of day and in the depths of night, through the savageness of winter and through the gentleness of spring, in the energy of youth and in the impotence of age, when health is merrily dancing in the blood, and when disease is eating up the strength, when death is in the lonely home, and when happy life encircles the hearth;—thus the wheel of labour would go round with the earth, and the children of industry, chained to its surface, must follow its ruinous circumvolutions, till, exhausted by unnatural efforts, they relax their hold, drop off, and suddenly disappear!

The worn-out wayfarer, finding no verdant resting place, and no house of entertainment to cheer him in his travel, must sink at length on the roadside and miserably perish. The delicate and the fragile would be speedily "crushed," by such a doom, "before the moth." Feeble constitutions, that with a seventh day's fostering care might eke out their residue of strength for many years, would be broken down with a sudden crash. Incipient diseases, which nature, invigorated by adequate rest, might overgrow, would be developed with a deadly rapidity. An intenser labour would be found a dreadful forcer of the seeds and rudiments of decay which are imbedded, more or less plentifully, in all of us. Under the vassalage of such a gigantic oppressor as unrestricted labour, earth would reek with the sufferings of her offspring, while the all-absorbing prayer of her millions would be for "Rest! Rest! Rest!" or the quiet slumber of the grave!

Oh, glorious Sabbath! almoner and nurse of health! we, the children of toil, flee to the shadow of thy protection. Thou standest beside us, like some guardian spirit, casting over us the shield of thine excellency, enfolding our jaded powers in thy sustaining arms, and saying to the encroaching tide of human selfishness, "Hitherto shalt thou come, but no further; and here shall thy proud waves be stayed." May thy bulwarks, notwithstanding all hostile assaults, stand strong as the everlasting hills, and be, in all coming ages, for a refuge and a covert to the children of men!

II. THE MERCANTILE ADVANTAGES OF THE SABBATH.

We have dwelt somewhat at length upon the physical benefits resulting from the observance of the Sabbath—contemplating it as the couch especially provided for the repose of the prostrated powers of industry; as a season eminently adapted to lure to the cultivation of all the graces and refinements of civilization, and as a provision designed to replenish the impoverished springs upon which an energetic condition of health and strength depends. But, besides these advantages, we believe it is capable of proof, that the suspension of all secular employment on the Sabbath contributes directly to the pecuniary interests of the working classes. This assertion will, perhaps, excite a momentary surprise in those who have have only viewed the subject with the eye of covetousness, and under the bias of a sordid heart. But, after pondering well the few rudimental thoughts we are about to submit, we think they will arrive at a thorough conviction of the soundness of this somewhat startling proposition.

For the sake of perspicuity, we shall divide the working classes of our country into two distinct branches—the two great arterial streams of production, that supply the necessities of the social body, and that create the wealth of the empire—

viz., our mechanics and our agricultural labourers; the former division comprehending our manufacturing operatives, our artificers, the workers in metals, and those following numerous other skilful crafts; and the latter branch comprising all farm servants, or individuals engaged in the production of food. Let us first view the subject in relation to the mechanical department of labour, by whose agencies we are furnished with all the external necessities and luxurious appendages of life; such as our apparel and all our personal ornaments, our dwellings, with all their garniture and utensils, and our libraries, with their literary stores.

The addition of the Sabbath to the established period of labour, would be attended by such consequences as are greatly to be deprecated by those whose hands are obliged to minister to their daily wants. They are these:—increased production, diminished consumption, a new stimulus to competition, and a reduction of wages. If these effects can be shown to be the legitimate fruit yielded by the secularization of the seventh day, we shall have done much towards winning for it a higher and warmer estimate on the part of many who have been wont to regard its observance with grudging aversion. If the former two results mentioned can be satisfactorily proved, the latter two, at least in a country like ours, depressed by a superabundant population, must inevitably follow.

I. INCREASED PRODUCTION.

The appropriation of the Sabbath to worldly occupations would be accompanied by increased production. That is, the fruit of our manufacturing exertions would be multiplied, just in proportion to the additional period of time devoted to labour. We are aware that this position is by no means certain—that it is based, perhaps, upon a fallacy. But then the alternative of relinquishing it would tell fearfully against the interests of our overtasked artisans, and would disclose such a state of things as Christians, philanthropists, patriots, and statesmen must alike deplore. However, as it is our intention to recur to this surmised objection again, we shall for the present assume the proposition to be sound, and give the working people of England the full benefit thereof. We shall now attempt simply to furnish some illustrations of its truth and validity. It is very clear that, all things being equal, the result of a man's industry who works six days or sixty hours, would be exceeded one-sixth by the result of seven days' or seventy hours' work per week. Only let this principle be expanded over the whole field of labour, and the aggregate result must be of the same nature as that in every individual case. Thus, then, it follows, that the present amount of manufactured stock, annually produced from the raw material, would be multiplied in the proportion of one-sixth, by the abstraction of the Sabbath from rest, which would be an increase equivalent to the sudden influx of nearly a million fresh operatives. Now the question for the working classes to consider is, would this increase of production be advantageous or detrimental to their interests? Would it promote their prosperity and independence, or conduce to their depression and servility? Would it tend to their progressive enrichment, or would it hang at length like a mill-stone about their necks, and drag them down to the depths of wretchedness? Is there a fair prospect of disposing of this immense excess of production? Are there markets available for this purpose? Are the ports of the world's commerce opening so rapidly to our trading enterprise, that there can be no reason to fear lest the supply should exceed the demand, lest our marts of merchandise should be glutted, and our warehouses crammed with unsaleable goods? Increased production, to any extent, could be attended by no evils, if consumption, domestic or foreign, kept pace with it. Do the signs of the times indicate the probable advent of such a state of mercantile prosperity? We trow not; but rather the reverse. So far, indeed, is it from being the case now, that we are in exactly the opposite condition. Our manufacturing industry already furnishes more than home necessities and foreign purchases combined can remuneratingly take off. Even now, during some portion of every year, tens of thousands of operatives are without emyloyment, or are compelled to abridge their hours of labour; whilst ever and anon some commercial crisis convulses the frame-work of society, drives multitudes forth from their cells of industry, and sends them drifting through the land—a famishing and beggared race! The effect of the secularization of the seventh day would be to augment and aggravate these terrible evils. But this is not all. It would lead to

II. DIMINISHED CONSUMPTION.

Storehouses gorged with surplus merchandise on the one hand, and a visible decline in the trading prosperity of a nation on the other, generally go together. The falling off, in the case we are assuming, would affect the staple commodities of business—food, apparel, and furniture; and this decline would result mainly from these two causes: —first, the non-employment of hundreds of thousands of men, women, and children, whose ordinary week-day operations would be superseded by the labours of the Sabbath, and who would, therefore, be incapacitated from obtaining any of the comforts, and but a few scanty morsels of the necessaries of life;—and a second source of this decline would exist in the diminished requirements of the working classes themselves for the indulgences of life. A population, despoiled of its holidays, and brutalized by ceaseless toil, would have little taste, and less leisure, for the acquisition of such things. The extension of our work over another day of the week would not create one new want, nor add any keenness to those already felt. No more food would be consumed in consequence, even with the sharpest appetite that labour could impart; for the Sabbath is, proverbially, with the thrifty poor, a day of feasting and good fare. The dwelling would boast of no richer garniture in consequence; no tasteful ornaments would be seen scattered about the room, when there would be no neighbours to drop in to admire the cottage tidiness. Alas! under such a system, how soon would the pride of housewifery be swept away, and nothing but the meanest utensils would remain to relieve the nakednesss of the domestic abode. And then, no more wearing apparel would be required in consequence. On the contrary, every inducement to procure showy and costly attire would be withdrawn. What millions then would never change the clothes that served them well enough for the drudgeries of life! It is impossible to calculate how great a portion of the working classes are indebted for their prosperity to the Sunday suits worn by the industrious millions. When we take into consideration the hands employed in manufacturing and beautifying the stuffs of which they are composed—in distributing and retailing them throughout the length and breadth of the land—and the everlasting stitch,

stitch, stitch, in fashioning them into vestments of elegance and beauty—we shall have some conception of the multitudes that draw their subsistence from this source alone.

Perhaps it may be urged against this view, that, if the lower orders did not purchase their dresses for Sabbath use, they would, nevertheless, procure them for other occasions. This would undoubtedly be the case, to some extent, among the better class of artificers, but would still, we apprehend, leave a serious defalcation in the demand for goods of other qualities. For it should be remembered that, with multitudes, the Sunday suit is quite distinct in material from the clothing required by them in following their respective crafts. Whether these festive habiliments are worn partly for the gratification of pride, is not now the question for us to discuss. We have here to consider it simply as an element of comparative mercantile prosperity, or depression—as a matter of pounds, shillings, and pence, in relation to the condition of the productive classes. And, so considered, the diminished consumption of the staple articles above mentioned, would reduce myriads of industrious families to destitution, and would recoil fearfully upon the cupidity of man.

III. INCREASED COMPETITION AND REDUCTION OF WAGES.

From a redundancy of production and an abated demand, must follow increased competition and reduction of wages. With less work to be performed, with a multiplying number of operatives, and with more time by one-sixth in which to exercise their callings, there would arise, of necessity, sharper emulations among those who have no property besides their hands and their health—nothing wherewith to support themselves and feed their families save their skill and labour. Men thus circumstanced, in order to secure some few crumbs at nature's table, would be found struggling desperately with their fellows, beating each other down to such a minimum of remuneration as would barely suffice for the necessaries of life. In a race where all the competitors could not win, each one would strive, at whatever hazards, to be himself the successful candidate: "Skin for skin, yea, all that a man hath will he give for his life." Now, it would be utterly impossible for an adequate rate of wages to be maintained amid the inroad of such evils upon the social economy. They must continue to sink lower and lower towards the point of utter penury and distress.

If the abrogation of the Sabbatical rest were not attended by the results we have predicted, then it would be in consequence of the two following facts:—viz., that seven days' uninterrupted labour is not more productive than six days' toil, supplemented by a day of rest; for it should be remembered, that time is but one of the many elements conducing to efficient and fruitful labour. Vigour of limb, buoyancy of spirit, and a joyous sense of freedom, are almost equally essential;—and again, that the mortality of our species, occasioned by this grinding system, would be increased to such a frightful extent, as continually to relieve the overgorged labour-market of its surplus hands. We leave the abettors of Sabbath abolition to decide on which of the horns of this dilemma they choose to be impaled.

But we must now offer a word or two respecting the bearings of the question on the husbandmen of our land. By the growth of the rural population, and the extensive displacement of manual labour by the introduction of machinery, the wages of this great body of our yokefellows have been already frittered down well nigh to a famishing point. But, miserable as is their condition at present, seven days' toil in every week would only serve to aggravate its horrors. A sixth portion of those at present employed, would be immediately expelled from the soil, billeted upon the large towns, and drafted into other occupations; or, disappointed in their most vigilant efforts thus to found for themselves a home by dint of honest industry, they would be compelled to take refuge within the precincts of some union-house; or else, by the pressure of their wants, would, under the influence of exasperated feelings, be goaded into the commission of crimes that would embitter all their days, and darken the once bright prospect of their eternal future. Whilst, at the same time, those who continued to plod at the employments of husbandry would soon discover that the pitiful sum, at which their sweat and strength were valued, would undergo no rise in consequence of their multiplied tasks: they would receive the same insulting pittance for seven days' labour that they had formerly received for six; for it is not the question, with many of their oppressors, what remuneration their hard services deserve, but upon how little of human fare the sons of the soil can labour and exist.

The foregoing considerations disclose to us this fact—that we do not need the Sabbath for mercantile, manufacturing, or agricultural pursuits, and that it is clearly the pecuniary interest of working men in particular to resist to the utmost all the encroachments of unnecessary labour upon that day. In volunteering their own services, either out of contempt for the day, or through a longing for unhallowed gains, or in countenancing the enthralment of their fellows, they are fighting against themselves, and plunging a dagger into the heart of their own prosperity. Rather let the whole community of labour, with unity of soul, rise to withstand every insidious attempt to wrest from them this *magna charta* of their rights, as the free creatures of God!

III. THE INTELLECTUAL ADVANTAGES OF THE SABBATH.

We have hitherto confined our illustrations of the value of this institution to its meaner uses—as a benevolent provision, conservative of the well-being and happiness of the body, and as an economical arrangement, conducive to the wealth and prosperity of the empire, but we now propose to advance a step further, and view the Sabbath in its adaptation to the higher attributes and more dignified relationships of man. He errs guiltily who regards the mechanic simply as a curious piece of mechanism, consisting of brains, and bones, and muscles, and nerves, endowed with extraordinary capabilities of labour, and who treats him precisely as he would any other piece of machinery, casting him off when no longer serviceable.

Man is a being of mysterious complexity, and he who, in subjugating his powers to menial tasks, overlooks or blinks this fact, commits a sacrilege upon his nature. Whilst there is nothing too low or groveling for him to stoop to, there is, at the same time, nothing too high to be attainable by his ambition. While his feet tread the ground, his brow fronts the sky. While his hands turn the sod, tug at the oar, or ply the loom, his soul, in its spiritual outgoings, may be roaming among the stars. The extremes of majesty and meanness thus meet in his nature. His perishing body establishes his affinity with the dust, while his indestructible spirit links him with the heavens. His limbs furnish him with instruments fitted for labour, but his intellect qualifies him for thought. The meanest serf, whose figure is bowed earthwards by the hardships of his lot, is invested with an immortal mind—all unhewn, and shapeless, and beautiless it may be, but still lying there, imbedded in the deep mines of his nature—dungeoned in darkness, peradventure, but still alive, looking hopefully through its bars, and struggling to be free—void and unfashioned now, but with capacities for treasuring up a vast fund of ideas—poor and talentless in its present state, but nevertheless a mint that may hereafter coin and give currency to its intellectual opulence—barren and birthless now, but containing in its womb the dormant rudiments of noble purposes, startling discoveries, beneficent deeds, or mighty revolutions. The annals of politics, the chronicles of science, and the archives of religion, bear witness to the bountiful upspringings of great and good men from these uninclosed wastes of humanity. Science can boast of its Kepler, its Ferguson, its Watt, its Newton, and its Stephenson; and literature can point, amidst innumerable others, to the names of Erasmus, Shakspeare, and Burns—all these having sprung from the loins of labour. Philanthropy has called some from the forge and from the anvil to the more blessed work of fusing hostile hearts and welding human sympathies. Religion, too, has ever selected her bravest and holiest champions from among the "common people." In primitive times she found her John, and James, and Peter, following the occupation of fishermen on the banks of the Galilean lake, and, taking them from thence, made them the apostles of her sublime revelations; and, in this late age of missions, she has drawn her most illustrious Christian heroes—her Martyn, her Brainerd, her Carey, her Williams, her Knibb, and her Moffat—from similar spheres of social obscurity, and sent them forth to humanize, regenerate, and redeem mankind.

Such being the inherent grandeur of man, even when found in the rudest condition and fulfilling the humblest functions, we may reasonably suppose that the Sabbath, being made expressly for man, whilst it ministered refreshment to his corporeal frame, would not overlook the higher necessities of his compound nature. Nor are we disappointed in these expectations. The Sabbath has a two-fold function to perform. It comes to give rest to matter and liberty to mind. Whilst it soothes the senses, it unleashes the spirit from its tether. It withdraws the hands from gold-gathering, that it may feed and feast the intellect with knowledge. It disinters the soul from the rubbish of earthly cares, and plumes it for higher converse and loftier studies. It favours inaction only so far as it shall contribute to the advancement of intelligence. Thus the Sabbath as clearly indicates that the working man has a mind, demanding to be exercised and enriched, as that he has a body sighing in its weariness for the sweet indulgences of rest. And how beautifully is it adapted to the former, as well as to the latter of these ends! It supplies the great desideratum of the artisan and husbandman's plodding existence—leisure for profitable reading and mental and moral culture. Its benign influences are eminently calculated to warm into life and nurse into maturity many of the finer attributes of mankind.

I. OPPORTUNITIES FOR PRIVATE STUDY AND REFLECTION.

The advantage of the Sabbath, as it respects the enlargement and fructification of the minds of the lower classes, is strikingly seen in the opportunities it affords for private study and reflection. The different callings pursued by the bulk of our working men engross nearly all their time, which they are thus compelled, by their indigent circumstances, to give in exchange for the means of subsistence. Where some few parings of time remain at the disposal of the sons of toil, they are generally so scattered, and occur at seasons when the corporeal powers are so prostrated, and the spirits so spent, as to be comparatively valueless, and passed in negligent musing. It must be admitted that such intervals of spiritless exhaustion are not calculated to predispose to intellectual effort, or to increase the hunger of the mind; but rather, where no deliberate resolve to excel has been formed, present strong inducements to waste them in scenes of excitement and sensuality. And, sad to tell, the garish and syren-voiced temptations of the world have prevailed, to a lamentable extent, in alluring our artisans and peasantry from the more solid pursuits of learning.

Now this great defect of the week is bountifully supplied by the boon of the Sabbath. It prescribes the ancient landmarks of labour, and incloses from the wide waste of common life an allotment sacred to the culture and growth of mind. A seventh portion of our time—fifty-two Sabbaths in every year, and ten years of Sabbaths, or 3650 days, in a life of threescore years and ten—is thus redeemed from secular pursuits, and becomes the especial property of mind. Oh, what intellectual riches would the Sabbath hours of an average life, wisely husbanded, enable us to hoard! How might we elevate our condition, dignify our characters, strengthen our virtues, and sweeten the bitterness of our lives, by a conscientious use of these oft-recurring opportunities! But, alas, how little is this princely blessing understood or appreciated by the working classes! How fearfully are its privileges abused, and its purposes perverted! Instead of works healthful in their tone and moral in their tendency, we find the reading multitude delighting in low and pernicious productions. Instead of reading books calculated to expand their intellect, and nourish in them great, and good, and god-like thoughts, we find among them works irreligious in their character, and designed to pander to the corrupt passions of human nature. In the place of the Bible may be seen the romance; in the place of the volume illustrating the works and ways of God, or descanting on the destiny of man, will be found the Sunday newspaper, consisting of the weekly off-scourings of a nation's depravity diligently raked together. This literary garbage is the mental aliment served up for Sabbath entertainment to tens of thousands of our working population. The issue of these messengers of impiety and immorality fluctuates between 50,000 and 100,000 weekly. What streams of corruption a prostituted press thus pours forth throughout the land, polluting the souls and vitiating the tastes of old and young, imparting morbid cravings to the minds of both sexes, and poisoning the nether springs of morality and religion. Where is the man who has risen from a low station to eminence of rank, or to commanding influence of mind, by feeding on such trash as this? Where shall we find the pioneer of liberty, the wrestler for human rights, the social regenerator, the original thinker, the conqueror of science, or the preacher of religion, who, in surmounting his early disadvantages, has not jealously husbanded the precious hours of the Sabbath? Never, until the working classes shall change their predilections, root out these literary tares from their homes, and spend a portion of the Sabbath in storing their minds with wholesome knowledge, will they realize the full advantages of the day, in relation to their intellectual development.

II. MEANS OF PUBLIC ORAL INSTRUCTION.

Besides the facilities thus supplied for the private acquisition of knowledge, the Sabbath also furnishes the means of public oral instruction. This provision is peculiarly valuable to the mass of the people, whose avocations and straitened circumstances necessarily exclude them from many sources of improvement accessible to others. It is pre-eminently the glory of the Sabbath. In England, Scotland, and Wales, about 35,000 buildings are flung open on this day for the impartation of instruction in morals and religion. About 40,000 minds, many of them gifted and powerful, have consecrated their talents to this work, and distribute on this day the fruit they have garnered up by the studies of the week. Everything in the nature and accompaniments of the day favours and aids their efforts. The cessation of business, the sudden enfranchisement of the thoughts from worldly thraldom, and the universal tranquillity that reigns around—all conduce to the success of the preacher's ministrations. But for the institution of these means, what multitudes of every generation must have passed to the grave ignorant of their responsibilities, their moral relations, and their destiny. The Sabbath abstracts the mind from carnal contacts, and keeps it from rooting itself altogether in the earth. It beckons the crouching spirit of the trader away from week-day scenes to higher and calmer regions.

The instruction dispensed on this day is of a character calculated to expand, refine, and sublimate the mind. It embraces a boundless range of topics, from the simplest elements of knowledge appreciable by the dullest intellect, to the most recondite mysteries that baffle the highest reason. It unseals the fountain-head of truth, in the nature of God. It unlocks the treasures of divine philosophy, in creation, in providence, and in redemption. It impresses into its sacred service whatever is beautiful in nature, grand in science, and instructive in art; whatever is pure in ethics, lovely in virtue, and sublime in revelation; whatever is monitory in the past, perilous in the present, and inspiriting in the future. It leads the mind backward to the ages before the flood, to the paradisaical state of man, to the origin of the universe, and thence to the vast solitudes of a past eternity; or it urges the shrinking spirit forwards, through the valley of the shadow of death—through the dark and populous empire of the grave—into the august presence of the Judge of all the earth—to the home of the beatified—to the pandemonium of the wicked—and outwards into the immensities of the everlasting future! It addresses itself to all the faculties and passions of the soul; it illumines the understanding, sobers the judgment, thrills the heart, softens the feelings, energises the conscience, and sanctifies the deepest affections of our mysterious nature.

The public instruction of the Sabbath teaches man also to understand himself—a study of supreme importance, and of intense interest, and one that should take precedence of every other. It is ever reminding him of his immortality, and giving premonitions of his latter end. Its lessons are suited to the changeful circumstances and experiences of his chequered history; it counsels him in his embarrassments, comforts him under his adversities, encourages him amidst his struggles, and strengthens him for the hour of temptation. It habituates the mind to the contemplation of all that is wonderful and glorious in God, and all that is hateful and terrible in sin; all that is divine in compassion, and victorious in love; all that is beautiful in holiness, and hideous in depravity;

all that is hallowing in truth, and pestiferous in error; all that is alluring in heaven, and revolting in hell. It is impossible to exaggerate the blessed effects resulting to the working classes from thus familiarizing their minds with sound scriptural views and holy Bible principles. Such instruction exerts a plastic power upon the character, and tends to make them more conscientious as servants, more patriotic as citizens, more peaceful as subjects; wiser as men, better as parents, and happier as Christians.

III. SABBATH-SCHOOLS.

The Sabbath-schools of our land afford another exemplification of the advantages of the Sabbath in relation to mind. These delightful institutions are mainly supplied with scholars from the families of the lower ranks of society. There are at the present time, according to a recent calculation,* not fewer than two millions of such children gathered every Sabbath day into these Christian nurseries; a large proportion of whom are employed through the entire week, and who, but for this expedient of Christian benevolence and zeal, would grow up in a state of barren ignorance. Here, then, we have a machinery, simple in its construc-

* See Edward Baine's Lecture on Education at Crosby Hall, Feb. 15, 1848.

tion, noiseless and unobtrusive in its operations, but nevertheless wonderful and far-reaching in its results. The ten thousand little streamlets glide unseen along the bed of society—the children and their teachers come and go from week to week—the busy world, meanwhile, taking no note of them; but a mighty and beneficent work is stealthily going on in secret. The fallow ground of two millions of minds is brought under the culture of spiritual husbandry.* The virgin soil of youthful hearts is turned up, and exposed to the warm breath of instruction. The seeds of evil germinating there—those indigenous to their nature, those shed upon them by a pernicious parental example, and those borne to them on the wings of every worldly influence—are sought out and carefully eradicated. Fresh sowings simultaneously take place, living germs of goodness are implanted, the stony heart is oft-times made ductile by tender treatment, the conscience is aroused, the intellect is dressed and fructified, an appetite for nutritious knowledge is created, and thus the work hopefully goes on.

Sometimes the green blade of promise speedily appears, the budding intellect expands its leaves, and the progressive life yields a rich crop of piety and usefulness. In other cases the springing is delayed. The golden grain seems to have perished

* A glorious band of 250,000 teachers are employed in the work of Sabbath-school tuition.—*Vide* Baine's Lecture.

in the ungenial bed to which it had been consigned. But no. Rank passions and luxuriant vices have only checked the precious seed, and retarded its growth. The living rudiments can never rot: they lie deeply earthed in the heart, entangled, perhaps, with the fibres of sins that root themselves there, awaiting a predestined day—an hour—a place—when and where they shall suddenly burst, with startling energy, into sight. It may be on the desolate rock, when the wreck is going down; it may be in the heart of a deep wilderness, or in the worse solitude of a crowded city, when no friendly face beams upon them; it may be in the grave-yard, in the day of desolation; it may be in the lonely chamber, in the dead of night; it may be in the dungeon, when crime is fully ripe; or it may be on the death-bed, when the judgment hour draws near! For on all these occasions, and in all these places, have the imperishable reminiscences of Sabbath-school instructions been suddenly revived, sometimes to communicate a glimmering hope of the Divine mercy, at others, to add fuel to the burnings of despair.

What rich fruitage has this blessed system already yielded! The Sabbath-school is a nursery of national righteousness. It has supplied men of integrity for responsible stations in society. It has, from year to year, replenished the church of God with new members. It has provided the ministry of our land with not a few of its most illustrious ornaments, and has given the first impulses of seraphic zeal to many of the most distinguished missionaries of modern-times. And who can compute the number of dormant minds it has quickened into activity—the fine intelligences it has opened and expanded, the memories it has stored with precious truths, the trailing virtues it has supported and invigorated, and the thriving vices it has withered, uprooted, and destroyed!

It is, moreover, the peculiar excellence of this educational system, that it not only developes intellect, but it developes it in a right manner. It does this, not by artificial stimulants, forcing a precocious and sickly growth, but by simply aiding the healthy action of nature. For it is not the abstract acuteness and capacity of any mind, but the proper application of its powers, that should be a matter of solicitude. A splendid intellect prostituted to the advocacy of error is a fearful curse, whilst the humblest talents, plighted to truth, and wisely directed, may prove an enduring blessing.

Had the Sabbath no other benefit of which to boast, than that of educating the incipient mind of the children of the working classes, it would be entitled to our warmest gratitude and commendation. Sabbath-school instruction is one of the most hopeful and influential of all labours, and in the present perilous times is emphatically required! If the wide under-growth of youthful mind be not carefully watched, and directed, in its earlier stages of development, small success will attend any subsequent efforts to improve it, when it has attained a dwarfed, misshapen, and stubborn maturity. If good impulses are not given to the rising intelligence of the labouring population in childhood, there is painful reason to fear that, in very many cases, the impressing season is irrevocably lost. Other teachers are in the field. Other influences are busy all around. Life opens up its beguiling scenes to the inexperienced eye. Harlotry lavishes its blandishments and weaves its snares. Scepticism insinuates its doubts. Profanity next approaches, flashing its witty jests and blasphemies. Enticements to dissoluteness and sensuality ply the unguarded victim on every side, till at length the time not spent in the duties of his calling is wasted in awful wickedness. Thus the fallen one becomes a wretched outcast from all good men. And thus minds that, with timely training, might have struggled into light and usefulness, become blasted by early neglect, and the fierce onset of earthly temptations.

But if youth will push its way to the brink of destruction, let us, nevertheless, fence the path with all possible resistances and obstructions. Since the road to ruin is so easy and congenial to the heart of man, let us lodge in his mind every principle that is calculated to retard his progress and damp his guilty ardour. This object is blessedly achieved by the Sabbath-schools of our country.

What a fund of blessing is thus hoarded up in the Sabbath! Its uses in relation to mind are not at present fully understood, for its rich available sources have never yet been half explored. The present Sabbath-school system, for instance, is but the embryo of a more perfect scheme for intellectual elevation hereafter to be disclosed.

IV. THE DOMESTIC ADVANTAGES OF THE SABBATH.

Besides numerous incidental and collateral benefits resulting from the advent of the Sabbath, in relation to the homes of the working classes, there are three great ends directly promoted by it that are worthy of special regard: it favours the cultivation of natural affection, it secures family fellowship, and it generates and fosters domestic piety.

I. UNDER THE AUSPICES OF THE SABBATH NATURAL AFFECTION IS NURTURED AND INCREASED.

The institution of families does not owe its origin to human ingenuity. God himself has grouped the human race in these miniature associations, and, by the refined instincts which he has implanted in their bosom, has, in all ages, and amidst all the confused comminglings of mankind, preserved this unique institution from destruction. The homes of men are the centres of nearly all the light and warmth that cheer the social world; the arks that shelter mankind from the raging tumults and storms of life; the cells where the loving and the loved hoard the sweet fruits of their reciprocal affection; the well-springs that supply mankind with the purest draughts of earthly happiness. Attachment to home is always strongest in the hearts of the virtuous and the good, whilst it will be found, that those who have abandoned themselves to sensualism and vice, have first learned to loathe the quiet joys, the chaste delights, and the gentle affections of the family circle.

All our natural affections are quickened by frequent and kindly domestic communion. The offices of love, the acts of devotedness, and the proofs of tenderness, constantly repeated among relatives mingling in the same dwelling, cannot but powerfully affect their emotional nature, and continue to weave, day by day, a chain of love around their hearts. The strength of this chain will depend, in a great measure, upon the frequency or infrequency of the intercourse subsisting between the respective members of the household. It is proverbial that absence tends to the estrangement of the heart, even from those claiming the closest kinship with us. Where our seasons of communion, therefore, only occur at lengthened intervals, or where they are hurried and embarrassed by the intrusion of care and anxiety, the bonds linking together the members of the family must of necessity be thereby relaxed and weakened.

These observations bring at once to our view the position of the working classes, in their respective families, as it respects the cultivation of those natural affections from which so large a share of their earthly enjoyments spring. During the days of labour the artisan or the husbandman is, to a great extent, an involuntary absentee from his home. He rises early in the morning, before the remainder of the family are up, and goes forth, like the sun, to perform his daily circuit of duty. If the scene of his operations happens to be near, he shows himself punctually at the hours of refreshment, partakes hastily of the family meals, and again disappears; but if, as is frequently the case, his sphere of labour be remote, then he returns no more to his fire-side till the evening is far spent, and when the children, or the sick wife perhaps, have retired to rest, whilst in very many instances the great distance of his employment will detain him from the bosom of his family till the broad shadows of the closing week are stretched across the land. This is the perpetual lot of millions of our toiling tribes. What opportunities, then, have they, in these swift visits to the domestic hearth, or in the drowsiness of evening exhaustion, to breathe sympathy or minister comfort to an ailing and suffering wife? What opportunities to win, by parental endearments, a lodgment

"The zone of Charity encompasses the household."

HEAVEN'S ANTIDOTE, p. 57.

in the hearts of their offspring? What leisure to sit under the shadow of the gourd their own hands have planted, and eat of its delicious fruits? If some provision had not been made to obviate the effects of this domestic deprivation, the families of the working classes generally would present a painful spectacle of mutual indifference and disaffection between husbands and wives, and of alienation between fathers and children; for when the natural affections, which mainly give birth to all the delights of home, are suffered to languish through neglect, there are no evils or distractions to which such households may not become a prey.

But the same benevolent Being who has, by certain constraining laws interwoven with our nature, clustered mankind in these little communities, has also, even in the most unpropitious circumstances, afforded facilities for promoting those refined instincts on the strength of which the happiness of the family institution chiefly depends. God has given to the sons of labour the Sabbath for a sacred possession. On this day the separations of the week do not take place; the dissociated are brought together into fellowship, the brother caresses the sister, the father lavishes his fondness upon the children, the husband tenderly greets the wife, and the zone of charity encompasses the household. The pulses of affection are quickened in every soul; each beholds his or her happiness imaged in the beaming countenances of all beside, and thus love ripens apace beneath the clear sunshine of the heart.

If the Sabbath fails to bring household harmony and interchanges of affection, as it does in too many cases, we must attribute it, not to any defectiveness in the provisions of the day, but to the prevalence of discordant passions in the bosoms of the members of the family. Their heart-strings are out of tune, consequently the music of domestic life is marred. The father is austere and despotic, it may be, or the mother is querulous and ill-tempered; in either case the green affections of childhood are blighted as soon as they appear. The husband is perhaps enslaved by intemperance, and robs his family to satiate his lusts; the down-trodden wife either upbraids him, or sullenly submits to her fate, and the slighted children learn to dread and recoil from their degraded sire. To such the Sabbath re-union brings no divine concord, no holy heart-communion, and thus ruthlessly does sin oftentimes blur the bright beauty of Sabbath homes, and neutralize the kind intents of Him who is alike the founder of families and of Sabbath days.

II. THE SABBATH SECURES TO THE WORKING CLASSES OPPORTUNITIES FOR DOMESTIC FELLOWSHIP.

This is but an amplification of the idea upon which we have already dilated. During the week by far the largest portion of their time is consumed amidst their coadjutors in toil, many of whom are comparative strangers to them, others are unworthy of their confidence and friendship, whilst the fellowship of not a few is decidedly distasteful and distressing. It imparts a double joy, therefore, to the intelligent and virtuous man, to be able to escape for a season from such contacts, and to find a temporary retreat in the bosom of a cheerful family. Here he can breathe freely, in an atmosphere untainted by the impurities that have surrounded him throughout the week. Here he can solace his soul with the sweet converse of those he loves. On this day he has time to imprint, line by line, lineament by lineament, an indelible image of himself on the hearts of his sons and daughters. On this day he has leisure to extract the honey of domestic happiness from the beauteous flowers bursting and blooming around him in the garden of his home. On this day he has opportunity to cultivate the affections of his children, by directing them towards worthy objects; to admonish them of their faults and follies, to point out the temptations to which they are exposed, to forewarn them, with a parent's earnestness, of the perils that beset their steps, to impregnate their minds with sound principles, to instil virtuous sentiments, to extirpate vindictive dispositions, to encourage the exercise of the intellect, and strive to exalt the moral sense, in short, to weed out of their natures whatever would prove detrimental to their happiness or usefulness, and at the same time to foster in them whatever might tend to improve their characters, or give stability to their future lives.

If this parental mission, to which the Sabbath peculiarly calls the heads of households, were but conscientiously fulfilled, what myriads of youth might be snatched from infamy, and what numbers of sorrowful parents, whose heads are prematurely bending to the grave, might spend a happy and extended old age beneath the family vine they had planted in their days of strength. But, in the most critical periods of their children's history, their minds and morals were neglected—left exposed to the sower of every sort of evil—and now, alas! they are harvesting a terrible retribution in the crimes and sufferings of their scattered offspring!

Contrasted with this dark picture, how blessed is the retrospect of a well-spent Sabbath in the family! What a sweet preparative for the struggles of the coming week! Where is the father who would not go forth on the Monday morning with a heart brimful with rapture to toil anew for his wife and children? And how often, as the hot dews of labour roll from his forehead, and his weary arms drop pithless by his side, will the swift thoughts of home rush over him, reviving him like new wine, and quickening all his flagging energies? The exertions of such a man, acting under such abiding impulses, cannot be otherwise than fruitful; and how precious should such fruits be esteemed, when cast into the family lap for the impartial use of all!

It is equally cheering to the matronly wife to be privileged, for one day in seven, to entertain her lord in the peaceful realms wherein she lives and reigns. Exiled to a great extent from her presence in the week, she ardently longs for the day when her husband shall fill the vacant chair beside the hearth, irradiate the cottage with his smiles, and delight her ear with that voice whose tones of tenderness whispered away her heart in the romantic days of her maidenhood.

But, if the communion of a well-ordered home be thus refreshing to parents, it is difficult to overrate the hallowing influence it exerts upon the minds of the rising members of the family. It helps to consolidate the virtuous formations of their characters. It preserves the guileless and unsuspecting from the fatal seductions that bestrew the highways of the world. It restrains those prurient desires that so often burn in the bosoms of the young, to rush into the world and into the blighting excitement that rages out of doors, and teaches them betimes that real happiness may be imbibed at the quiet cistern of domestic enjoyments, but never from the turbid currents of a dissipated life.

And then, this influence is as lasting as it is beneficial. The recollections of a happy home will cling to the young adventurer when his turn comes to plunge into the wild waters of a turbulent world. In the case of him who is under the sway of virtuous principles, these sacred remembrances will never lose their power; whilst in the case of him who has swerved from the path of rectitude, the Sabbath counsels of a serious father, and the fervent pleadings of a pious mother, will vibrate upon his ear amid the guilty excesses of a profligate career. The earliest impressions of home are generally the deepest, and the last to be effaced; and where these are of a pleasing and salutary character, they will often act like an anchor, in steadying the heart of the young sinner, and preventing him from driving headlong on the rocks of destruction! But there is yet another aspect in which the domestic advantages of the Sabbath may be viewed.

III. THE SABBATH AFFORDS FACILITIES FOR THE PROMOTION AND EXERCISE OF FAMILY PIETY.

The ordinary work-days of most of our operatives are necessarily so engrossed by their out-door occupations, and the time consumed in going to and fro, that, whatever their inclinations may be, they seldom have opportunity to indulge in the offices of family devotion. Business, as now conducted, is so thoroughly worldly in its spirit and requirements, and so greedy of every moment it can wrest from its slaves, that no space is left, between the rising and the setting sun, for the pious labourer to assemble his household around the domestic altar. His meal-times barely suffice to enable him to reach his home, to appease the appetites of nature, and to retrace his steps again. Thus the devout workman, however his soul may pant for a brief daily season which he may consecrate to the social exercises of religion, finds himself irresistibly borne onwards by the tide of human selfishness, and compelled to conform to many of the customs and restrictions imposed by the ungodly.

But here again, as elsewhere, the mercy of Heaven interposes on behalf of its vexed children. Every seventh day that breaks upon the groaning world publishes liberty to these lamenting captives. The rich banquet which this day spreads, atones, in some measure, for the spiritual scarcity of the week. On the Sabbath the perusal of the Scriptures may be resumed, the re-united household, free from the inquietudes and claims of secular duties, may meet for praise and prayer around the throne of grace; the well-matched pair will take sweet counsel together, and of the Lord; the inquisitive children, gladdened at their father's sojourn among them, will drink from his lips the words of sacred instruction; friends and kindred, dropping in, will fraternise with the family in their communings with each other and with heaven, and go away bearing a rich blessing in their souls; songs of rejoicing and canticles of praise will resound through the templed cottage, whilst the foretastes of heavenly bliss will often ravish the hearts, and the foreshadowings of a coming glory will gleam upon the countenances, of its happy inmates. Nor will the public ordinances of divine worship interrupt this holy fellowship. An intelligent and earnest piety in the rulers of the family will generally so contrive, as that most, if not all, of its members may repair in company to the house of God, and there celebrate divine mercy with the great congregation of Israel.

Such are some of the inestimable privileges which the Sabbath institution guaranties to the families of the working classes. It requires, therefore, but a glance to perceive the deranged and godless state to which the repeal of the Sabbath law would reduce them. The natural affections of the lower orders would thereby be blunted, and a diminished interest in each other's well-being would ensue, in consequence of the infrequency and hastiness of their family intercourse. The several members of the same household would grow up in strange and freezing apathy towards each other. The children would seldom see the father, except for a few hurried minutes, and then it would be when he is chafing beneath the labour-yoke, and when his eye is continually roving to the admonitory hands of his watch—a time not at all calculated to encourage the reciprocities of paternal and filial love. The father, too, on his part, never having a few consecutive hours of leisure, to enable him to explore the mine of household treasure which he nominally possesses, would soon feel the chain of labour drag as heavily as his dead heart within him, while the brawny arm of energy, and the soul of enterprise, would flag, because the inspirations of love were wanting. For, where ambition, or covetousness, or emulation stimulates one to indefatigable effort, love impels thousands on in the fierce races of human industry. Think of this state of things everywhere existing among the working classes—think of homes divested of their attractions—think of the bonds of sympathy between the closest kindred universally relaxed—think of the strong affinities of nature which, for lack of adequate domestic fellowship, are dying out of human hearts—think of hard labour, thus deprived of its elastic spring, going on with sluggishness and languor, for who would toil, and sweat, and "grind the bones out of his arms," without a powerful motive?—and what motive is sufficiently strong to urge millions of our yokefellows to menial offices all their lives, save necessity to provide for themselves, and love towards those dear ones who have a natural claim upon their services?—think of the consequences that would ensue from the withdrawal of this mainstay of the industrial habits of the people, and infer therefrom the inexpressible advantages accruing to innumerable family groups, and to society at large, from the maintenance of the Sabbath from all secular and carnal innovations.

The extinction of the Sabbath, moreover, as a day designed to be especially devoted to religious pursuits, must lead to the extinction of domestic piety; and wheresoever piety shall cease to have a voice and an altar in the house, it will simultaneously cease to have an embodiment in the church, and an existence in the world. Were religion, with its angel-retinue of graces, to be thus banished from our earth, godlessness and impiety, with their demon-throng of attendant evils—oppression, extortion, discord, hatred, revenge, blood-thirstiness, and every species of sensuality that can debase the human form—would reign and riot unchecked among mankind! Between us and a catastrophe so dire stands the Sabbath day, whose seemingly frail barriers were originally built, and whose dilapidations from age to age have been repaired, by the hands of a divine artificer.

V. THE MORAL ADVANTAGES OF THE SABBATH.

This is one of the most solemn phases of the subject. It may be viewed very differently by different minds. The dominant mood of the ruminator is likely to darken or illumine the steps by which he reaches his conclusion. We believe that the beneficial influence of the Sabbath on the interests of morality can be triumphantly established. In the right dedication of the day is locked up all its hoarded blessedness. Used in accordance with its institutional laws, it is birthful of unmingled good. Desecrated to dissipation, wasted in the chase of vanity, or pawned for unblessed gains, it entails a terrible and an accumulating curse.

I. THE SABBATH FAVOURS MORALITY, INASMUCH AS IT INCULCATES THE PRACTICE OF MORAL DUTIES, AND GIVES FREE SCOPE TO THE EXPRESSION OF THE MORAL VIRTUES.

In the fulfilment of these functions it wages a vigorous war against the reigning spirit of the work-day world. The mandates of Christianity, thundered across the Sabbath stillness, are calculated to arrest the demoralizing mania of worldly grasping, and bring men to a reflective pause. The prescriptions of the gospel, which are being constantly republished under the sanctions of the Sabbath, are utterly at variance with the selfish maxims and greedy impulses of a trading community. Whilst, on work-days, the competitions of industry and the contentions of trade are continually fomenting jealousies and animosities between mankind, the Sabbath seeks, by its lessons of forgiveness, to reconcile and fraternise the alienated. Whilst, throughout the week, prosperous extortioners overreach their neighbours, and wring the materials of wealth out of the stinted poor, on the Sabbath they are confronted by some stern messenger from the avenger of oppression, and into their tingling ears is pealed the royal law of love, "Do unto others as you would that others should do unto you." Amidst the weekly drudgeries or hirelingship, the factitious disparities of station, and the inequalities of lot, stand out in dismaying prominence, causing heart-burnings among the more dependent classes: in the eye of the Sabbath all men are regarded as equal—the wide chasms that yawn between the different sections of society are closed, and class enmities and feuds are abated. The frequent hardships and indignities inflicted upon the labouring poor breed bitterness in their souls, and prompt them to reprisals: the Sabbath not only manumits them from these galling impositions, but teaches them to love, to forgive, and to do good unto those who despitefully use them. In the desperate struggles which the week witnesses for earthly distinction and aggrandizement, the rights of others are frequently trampled on with reckless temerity; competing rivals are mercilessly over-ridden, and thus an awful disregard of the charities of life is propagated: the Sabbath lifts up its standard against this prevalent spirit of selfishness, reproves all such encroachments on the primary rights of man, and pleads the cause of the injured and distressed. All the commercings of week-day life nourish the selfism of man, whilst the Sabbath, on the contrary, appeals to, and seeks to bring forth, the benevolence of his nature. The whole gist of secular occupations is to tempt man to sacrifice others, as far as is needful, for the attainment of his own private ends, whilst the scope of the Sabbath is to prevail upon him to sacrifice himself for the benefit of his fellows, whether by ministering with his gold to their physical necessities, whether by extending a helping hand to the unfortunate and sinking, whether by exploring the outlying settlements of social darkness and degradation, and afterwards calling the attention of the world to their humiliating revelations, whether by consecrating his gifts to the general advancement of his species, whether by going meekly from hovel to hovel, and from cellar to garret, breaking the bread of truth, and handing round the cup of comfort to the ignorant and the unhappy, or whether, if needs be, by pouring out his blood and life, a libation on the altar of human happiness. For, while dissuading from gainful frauds and worldly greediness, as ignoble in themselves, and trenching on the dues of others, the Sabbath also summons the sons of men to all these moral duties and disinterested services.

The day that inculcates these obligations likewise teems with opportunities for their discharge. The Sabbath is the fulcrum on which the lever of the Gospel mainly rests. It fosters every noble enterprise, and promotes all that is truly good, and great, and hopeful in man. It is earthly life filtered of its dregs. It is the cream of time. It closes the ordinary outlets of cupidity, and directs the activity of men into a thousand holier channels. It gives abundant time for well-doing. It works out, too, a generous willinghood of heart. It breaks down alike the opposing barriers of business and the more stubborn aversions of mind. It empties the warrens of the world, and swarms the vineyards of the church. It clears the shops, the mines, and the factories of the land, and, with their inmates, peoples human homes. It flings wide open the doors of opportunity to all, and thus prepares a harvest for the Christian reaper's sickle. It gathers the younger children from the school, or from the mill, the grown sisters from the seamstress's, the elder brothers from the desk, or from the field, the father from the workshop, the barn, or the mine, and the mother from her cottage drudgeries, and groups them all around the cheerful fireside.

All trading, world-made distinctions are now effaced. Men appear no longer as miners, as weavers, as masons, as ploughmen, or as builders. The Sabbath recognises them alone as men—as responsible beings—moral agents—candidates for immortality—the subjects of a retributive government—and the objects of impartial, divine benignity and grace. How solemn are the aspects of human nature that the Sabbath thus discloses! What a spectacle of hidden majesty it enshrouds! How silently it tears away all that is merely adventitious in man, and bares to view a world of spirits, awing the eye that surveys them in all their grandeur and vast interests! A world of spirits! shrined in flesh! guested in tabernacles of dust! self-sunken in abysses of depravity! borne down by heavy tasks of toil! all the radiant beamings of their high destiny shut in, or else extinguished! This infinite region of spiritual existence would have remained well nigh unknown but for the Sabbath, for when would despotic labour have voluntarily suspended its mean pursuits to explore its mysteries? When would avarice or ambition, for ever on the drive, have found leisure to study its sublime secrets? To the mass of men, rolled onward on the restless surges of a Sabbathless life, this illimitable world of spiritualism must have continued unknown, save when some stray glimmerings of its glories might occasionally struggle through an opening in the gloom wherewith their nature and destiny were enwrapped. Too contented as men are to linger in the outer courts of the temple of the universe, were it not for the rending of the veil, by the hand of the Sabbath, few men would have had the inclination to enter within the sacred penetralia of their being. But, glorious to tell, the Sabbath has torn off man's earthly disguises, raised the vassal of labour from his abject posture, and proclaimed aloud his original dignity and worth. How magnificent the field, and how boundless the scope, thus opened to the moral student and the Christian husbandman!

II. THE SABBATH FAVOURS MORALITY BY THE DIVERSIFIED TALENTS IT ENLISTS, AND THE INNUMERABLE AGENCIES IT ORGANIZES, IN ITS SERVICE.

The blessed release which the seventh day brings, and the sacred leisure which it bestows, have induced the benevolent and the good of our world to seize upon these facilities and turn them to the highest profit and advantage of mankind. On this day talents that had been buried in the world, through lack of a fitting sphere for their exercise, are disinterred and employed. Sanctified gifts, that are often compelled to lie barren through the week, are fruitful in usefulness on the Sabbath. On this day the pent-up goodness of the world obtains vent, the cramped energies of philanthropy find enlargement, while all the holier sympathies of men for their erring and outcast brethren are evoked. Exhortations and teachings, which it would affront the children of the world to thrust upon their attention during the week, may now be fittingly and more effectually addressed. Compassion, that can find an outlet only for its yearnings whilst under the bonds of secular engagements, may now freely go forth in search of the wretched objects of its commiseration.

As soon as the golden gates of the Sabbath are flung back, what angel-shapes of good rush in upon the world! As the day advances, what glorious legions are going up to assail the evils reigning in the earth! What a holy host of messengers are running to and fro! What lips are dropping with divine instruction! What a multitude of voices, attuned by love, are exhausting all the arts of eloquence! What vehement appeals, gushing from full souls, are everywhere smiting the ears of apathy, riving the consciences of the guilty, and fusing the petrified hearts of the wicked! On this day, in our own land, not fewer than from 30,000 to 40,000 recognized ministers are reasoning, pleading, and expostulating with millions of their fellow-men, composed of all shades of character and of all grades of guilt. About the same number of exhorters and evangelists are itinerating the villages, the hamlets, and the more outlying portions of the population. Home missionaries, city mission agents, visitors of the sick, and Bible readers, in abundance, are permeating the channels of obscure life, and purifying the dregs of society with the vital elements of truth. Not less than 250,000 Sabbath-school teachers are seeking to disinfect the minds, and to mould and sanctify the characters, of two millions of the rising generation, that are soon to supplant their fathers. Besides these more public and organized efforts in the service of morality and religion, what earnest lessons are being instilled in the retirements of home; mothers indoctrinating their offspring with virtuous sentiments and godly precepts, and shedding tears of solicitude upon indurated hearts, and fathers inculcating upon the impatient temperament of their sons the lessons of wisdom they have acquired in the suffering school of adversity and experience.

Now the end and aim of all these simultaneous efforts is, so far as they have respect to the present world, to promote the interests of public morality. And only think for a moment of the stupendous, deep, and permanent influence which this weekly concentration of holy forces must exert upon the general mind. How it emboldens virtue and abashes vice! How it chastises arrogance and rewards humility! How it opens the heart of niggardliness, and quickens the pulses of benevolence! How it dashes the chalice of sinful pleasure with bitterness, and discovers its dregs of gall! How it bridles furious passions, and slakes the fires of consuming lusts! How it hedges with briars and thorns the ways of wickedness, and illumines with honour the paths of justice and uprightness! How many retire to their evening rest, as the stricken deer to its mossy couch, with the arrows of remorse rankling in their hearts! And what numbers on the succeeding morning cross the Sabbath frontiers, and pass into the world with the dread voice of God vibrating on their ears, and the thunders of his anger reverberating through their souls!

But, in the position we have taken, we are open to the objection that, whilst the Sabbath brings a vast accession to the moral forces ordinarily at work upon the world, it at the same time lets loose upon society an amount of demoralizing influences, fearfully predominating over all that is healthful and good. It will be retorted, that the suspension of employment which we demand for the working classes may, by multitudes of our countrymen who possess no religious predilections, and who are conscious of no intellectual cravings, be abused to their own injury and to the infliction of serious evils upon society. Idleness, it may be alleged, is the parent of mischief. Authorized leisure, falling into the hands of the profligate, will be sure to be spent in wantonness and rioting; drunkards will waste it in debauchery; courtezans will find a disengaged population peculiarly susceptible to their blandishments; the devotees of pleasure will convert it into a carnival of delight: and thousands, prompted by a lust for gain, will abet these practices and pander to these vile tastes. The priests of Bacchus will be driving a flourishing trade in the myriad temples of their god; tea-gardens, abounding with music and dancing, hot excitement, and all the witcheries of sin, will present their enticements to the young; whilst the proprietors of steamboats, and the directors of railways, will increase their dividends, by ministering to this feverish passion for lawless liberty and joy.

It is too true. We admit it all. Facts impart a mournful plausibility to this objection. But we deny the inference which the adversary of the Sabbath would draw from it. Because the sacred leisure which God gives to man is thus perverted from its exalted uses, must we then chain men down, like condemned galley-slaves, to everlasting drudgeries, in order to keep them out of the reach of temptation? Must we bandage their limbs and stultify their minds, to prevent the gratification of their low-born desires and the spread of their contagious example? Are we to deny them the freedom and rights of men lest they should abuse them to licentiousness and immorality? Nay, men must be dealt with as moral agents, and not as tools in the hands of purblind expediency. The Sabbath is a test of moral bias. It leaves men to the spontaneous outgoings of their nature. It discovers of what sort they are. The Gospel wars not so much against particular forms as it does against the principle of evil. It directs its remedial measures not so much to the symptoms as to the central seat of the disorder. It is not chiefly engaged in plucking and crushing the poisonous fruits as fast as they ripen, but fetches its heavy blows at the roots of the upas tree. For, be it remembered, that whatever luxuriant evils may be thrust to the surface on the Sabbath, they were previously already in existence, sprouting in the seed-bed of the heart, and waiting only for favourable circumstances to accelerate their development and nurse them to maturity. The Sabbath, therefore, does not give birth to the many baneful evils that spring up and flourish beneath its brightness, any more than the sun can be said to create the deadly hemlock and nightshade, or the hurtful tares, that are nourished from the fountain of its splendour. All violent, arbitrary, and oppressive attempts to hinder the desecration of the Sabbath must fail. The cure will be only skin-deep. If every outlet for the virus of society be closed, the raging malady will be driven deeper into the social constitution. Any panacea, to be efficacious, must go to the very core of human nature, and purge its innate rottenness.

Thus the friends of morality and of the Gospel have abundant incentives to exert themselves. Let them still continue bravely to breast the dark surges of the world's wickedness. Their Sabbath mission is pre-eminently aggressive. To stand still is impossible, amid the rush, and restlessness, and roar of the human sea. By presenting a broad front, and by a firm evangelical bulwark alone, can the strong tide of worldliness be turned, and progress be achieved. Whilst the Sabbath peculiarly exposes the irreligious and the vicious to the appliances of hell, it likewise opens a sublime sphere for Christian labour and enterprise, which, without it, we might seek in vain. On every Sabbath the weekly controversy is renewed, between God and Satan, between truth and error, between virtue and vice, between loyalty and treason! The singular moral phenomenon is seen of light struggling for ascendency in the midst of darkness, and of a redeemed race seeking to imbue the corrupted mass of men with the principles of holiness and love. Thus, from year to year, the universal battle rages on between the emissaries of heaven and hell—between Michael and the dragon; but, through all the vicissitudes and evolutions of the church, the tide of public morality is ever mounting higher and higher.

It is true this is not at all times apparent. There are, ever and anon, seasons of depression and of temporary retrogression. The religious progress of a nation is subject to fluctuations, as well as its trade and commerce. The present period, for instance, is a fearful crisis in the social and spiritual condition of our country. Practical religion seems long to have been ebbing; it is indeed at its neap-tide. The bonds of public morals are alarmingly relaxed. Still we are anxiously looking for the return of a spring-tide of prosperity. Meanwhile, if we take an average standard of comparison, we shall find that we have advanced considerably above the highest point of past times. Besides, many of the popular sins which we most pungently deplore, are such only as seen in the purer and clearer light which Christianity sheds increasingly around us.

But a solemn responsibility rests upon all Christian people! Let them, especially at this critical juncture, beware of throwing any stumbling-blocks in the way of the general reformation of Sabbath manners, and of the moral and spiritual regeneration of society. All now depends upon the energy and perseverance of the good; for if the Sabbath, through their supineness and unfaithfulness, should be partially abolished, and spent in labour or in licentiousness, how then could the agents of good reach the people?—how could the machinery of salvation be successfully worked? All men—and our working population in particular—would be subjected to evil influences only, and that continually.

VI. THE RELIGIOUS ADVANTAGES OF THE SABBATH.

These are so manifest and unequivocal, that, but for the completion of the argument, their consideration might well be omitted. Forming, however, as they do, the culminating point in the subject, they claim a succinct notice at our hands. A record of them is as essential to the perfection of the subject as the head-stone is to the finish of an edifice. The higher we have ascended into the Sabbath's lofty territory, the purer has the air become, the more has the prospect widened, and the richer have been the clusters of blessings we have plucked. And now we have at length reached its divine heights, and stand midway betwixt earth and heaven, from whence the mists of human woe are seen floating at our feet, the tumults of earth dying away into a confused murmur, whilst upwards the enraptured gaze is riveted upon the scenery of the opening skies. The benefits of the Sabbath are commensurate with the heights and depths of man's nature, and the lengths and breadths of its necessities. The mind of man is not capacious enough to hold all the benefactions that the Sabbath pours forth; neither can the dower which it confers upon the intellect, nor the contributions it makes to domestic enjoyment, exhaust the treasures that it holds in store. It reserves its noblest blessings for the spirit of man, in the exercise of its highest prerogatives and in its most dignifying relations.

Let us now, with as much brevity as possible, advert to a few spiritual advantages of supreme moment, accruing from the observance of the Sabbath, so far as they bear upon the temporal interests of mankind.

I. THE SABBATH IS THE CHIEF MEDIUM FOR PRESERVING AND PERPETUATING THE KNOWLEDGE AND WORSHIP OF GOD IN THE WORLD.

A correct conception of God, together with veneration for his character, is of infinite importance to mankind. It constitutes the best safeguard of states. It imposes a salutary check upon rulers, and it inspires the governed with respect for the majesty of law. It is essential to the preservation of morality; virtue would perish without it. It is indispensable to the maintenance of society. It is the basis of all true brotherhood. It reveals the origin and guaranties the possession of human rights. It is the most ennobling element of human character. It is at once the most simple and sublime, the most necessary and stupendous, of all studies. It keeps man, on the one hand, from degenerating into the brute, whilst, on the other, it advances him to a state of intellectuality and spiritualization. It is requisite for the cultivation of the religious sentiment in man; and without such development his nature is but half disclosed—his latent character but half expressed.

But the knowledge of God, and therefore all the precious benefits resulting from it, depend upon the sanctification of the Sabbath. Wherever the Sabbath does not exist, there is no religion, no intelligent homage. Man utterly forgets God, and God punitively hides his face from man. "The moral world becomes a desert, where life never springs and beauty never smiles. Putrid with sin, and stupefied with ignorance, the soul of man loses its rational character, and prostrates itself before idols, stocks, and stones. To these man offers his prayers, his praises, and his victims; to these he sacrifices his offspring; and to these he immolates the honour of his wife. A brutal worshipper of a brutal god, he hopes for protection and blessing from the assumption of every folly and the perpetration of every crime."* A population wronged of their Sabbaths, and enslaved by ceaseless toil, cannot possibly retain any spiritual or exalted conceptions of the Supreme Being. Besides, having no adequate opportunities for the acquisition of defined ideas on this momentous subject, the inevitable tendency of a servile destiny is to generate gross and derogatory notions, corresponding with their own debased condition. With the spiritual portion of their nature virtually cancelled, and well nigh every diviner lineament effaced, how can they think of God—if they think of Him at all—otherwise than as such an one as themselves? The popular religion of a people is an infallible index to their character and habits. Where low and obscure notions of God are entertained, we shall find them indicative of an ignominious condition, of a rude disposition, of an entombment of mind, of an utter prostration of all moral majesty. Whereas, where the most luminous, vivid, and profound conceptions of the Divine Being abound, we find a people distinguished by all that is refined in manners, urbane in disposition, and ennobling in pursuits; renowned for their scientific at-

* Dr. Dwight.

tainments, for the achievements of their genius, and the beneficence of their virtues.

II. NECESSARY FOR THE DIFFUSION OF CHRISTIANITY.

The Sabbath is imperatively necessary for the diffusion of Christianity. These are natural and hereditary allies. There is a divine kinship between them. The hand that smites the one insults and wounds the other also. Their success or defeat is correlative. They live or die together, sharers in one indissoluble fate. Voltaire keenly felt this, and gnashed his teeth in impotent rage. His malignant attempt to subvert Christianity signally failed, through his inability to abolish the Sabbath, and stifle the immortal yearnings of men's hearts for its sacred privileges and immemorial usages. The Sabbath, every week, opens the vast temple of creation, for the celebration of solemn worship, gathering adoring hosts around the enshrinements of mercy, and repeating, throughout its spacious courts, with ten thousand times ten thousand voices, the transforming story of the Cross. Christians! we urgently appeal to you. Shall this temple of praise—this pavilion of peace—be closed by the suppression of the Lord's Day? Shall the throne be forsaken, and the altar overturned? Shall the anxious crowds, that have been wont to come up to the solemn feasts of Zion, be turned back upon the desert places of a bleak and bitter world? Shall the rehearsals of the Song of Redemption cease, and, instead thereof, the groans of those who are wrestling with a slavish lot be heard ascending to the ears of the Lord of Sabaoth? Shall Christianity be arrested in the very midst of its enterprises, and hunted from the world ere its benign mission has been half accomplished? Is the highest manifestation of benevolence to succumb to the hostile combinations of human selfishness? Is piety to be trampled under foot by impiety? Is religion to be supplanted by atheism? Is guilt to go pining to the grave without the discovery of its expiatory sacrifice? Is the day coming—are we already entering its shadows—when the great Teacher and loving Saviour is to be suffered to go in and out among his purchased ones no more? Oh, men of God! awake and bestir yourselves to a right appreciation of the Sabbath! If you love Christianity—if you believe it to be of God—if you believe it to be the only means of restoring man to his Maker's allegiance, likeness, and fellowship—then diligently guard its imperiled treasures by upholding the bulwarks of the Sabbath. Every profane foot that trespasses upon its sanctity—every additional burden of duty imposed upon our operatives, our cabmen, our domestics, and railway servants—every effort to relax the stringency of its requirements—every attempt to popularise it by the introduction of continental licentiousness—

must be jealously watched and strenuously resisted. If the working orders can but be brought to despise or undervalue this blessed birthright, it will not be long before it is either forcibly wrested from them, or bribed away for some alluring morsel. In that melancholy day of their whole nature's nakedness, may God have mercy on them! for the pity and the help of man will not avail!

III. THE SABBATH GUARANTIES A SEASON FOR UNMOLESTED ATTENTION TO THE SOUL.

If the body needs intervals of repose—if the mind requires the redemption of opportunities for its improvement—how much more does the soul sigh for a kind recognition of its claims! And the Sabbath-day does pay homage to man's immortal spirit. It enshrines his dignity. It memorializes his primitive excellence and glory. It foreshadows his brilliant or his appalling destiny. It is the ancient and enduring witness to the undiminished worth of his sullied nature. It is that strip of our time which especially links earth with eternity; which dwindles the present to a mere speck, in the vastness of that futurity which it discloses. In many senses it is a type and symbol of heaven. It repeals, to a great extent, for the time being, the invidious distinctions of society. It unsceptres the master, and denudes the hireling of the badges of his servitude. Opulence cannot buy up its spiritual blessings, whilst poverty operates as no disqualification for its favours. Its smiles are as sweet in the wood-side hut as in the apartments of the marble palace. It pays no obsequious deference to learning, rank, or worldly power; and it offers no insulting slights to millions whom the world disdains. Its glances go far deeper than the rags or robes, the roughness or the polish, of the outer man. It is sent as a messenger to the godlike guest lodging in all men's bosoms, and proclaims, in the ears of all alike, the abstract grandeur and preciousness of the human soul.

On this day, the merchant, the trader, the husbandman, and the mechanic, can yield up their whole thoughts to the momentous matters of salvation, and give wing to their aspirations after eternal life; while at the same time they enjoy the satisfying conviction, that no temporal duties are thereby neglected, nor any deranging check interposed to the ordinary courses of business. Free from the irritations incident to secular pursuits, here is a season eminently adapted for celestial contemplation, for the study of the heart, for the perusal of the Scriptures, for the special exercise of spiritual gifts and graces, for intercession on behalf of others, and for an undistracted attendance on the public solemnities of religion.

"God has anointed this day with the oil of gladness above all its fellows. What the sun is among the planets—what the market-day is to the tradesman—what a fair wind is to the sailor—what the tide is to the waterman—that the Sabbath-day is to the soul. Augustine calls it the 'Queen of days.' It is the great market-day of heaven, when starving souls may take in, and lay up, provision for the rest of the week, yea, for eternity itself. Blot out this day from the calendar of the Christian, and all that remains would be cloudy and cheerless."*

IV. ITS OBSERVANCE THE BEST PREPARATIVE FOR THE VICISSITUDES OF THE WEEK.

The sanctification of the Sabbath is the best preparative for the vicissitudes of the week. It instils accurate views of the world. It disenchants the imagination of the spells of the great delusion. It sends us forth into the highways and bypaths of life, with watchful eyes, an engarrisoned heart, and an attempered spirit. It dignifies our daily duties, instead of suffering us to be undignified and debased by them. It corrects our estimate of temporal prosperity, and enables us to enjoy its favours with moderation and meekness; whilst it unstings the privations of adversity, and helps us to bear them with magnanimity. It superinduces a mood of mind and tone of feeling, calculated to blunt the poignancy of human griefs, to break the shocks of

* Sherman's Plea for the Sabbath.

worldly disappointments, and to preserve some cheering beams of hopefulness amidst the darkest day. It imparts equanimity to the disordered passions—acts as an anodyne to the feverish excitement of the mind—smooths the asperities of the temper—and thus, by restoring the functions of self-control, aids us in triumphing over the adverse circumstances of life. It forewarns and forearms for the conflict between grace and corruption; it rouses the mind into a defiant and repellent attitude to meet the onsets of temptation; and it makes the blackest cloud of impending trial transparent with divine light, as we enter upon its shadows. Its counsels are generally conducive to our worldly interests, to social elevation, to independence of character, and to an honourable reputation. And this it achieves, not by fostering the spirit of sordid gain, but by enforcing the claims of godliness, whose prerogative it is, to have "the promise of the life that now is, as well as of that which is to come." We cannot conclude this part of our subject better, than by adducing the testimony of the eminent Lord Chief Justice Hale, respecting the salutary influence of the Sabbath on the engagements of the ensuing week. He says: "I have found, by a strict and diligent observation, that a due observing of the Lord's Day has ever had joined to it a blessing upon the rest of my time, and the week thus begun has been blessed and prosperous to me; and, on the other side, when I have been negligent of the duties of this day, the rest of the week has been unsuccessful and unhappy to my secular employments, so that I could easily make an estimate of my success through the week by the manner of my passing this day."

Although the demonstration of the divine origin of the Sabbath forms no part of our contemplated design, still it is by no means extraneous to the scope of this essay. If the foregoing views be correct, they must force on every candid mind the conviction, that the redemption of a seventh portion of our time from common uses, and its preservation from age to age, despite the encroachments of human hostility, impiety, and cupidity, does not arise from a mere conventional compact of society; but rather that it exhibits marks of a more profound and far-seeing wisdom, and tokens of a higher and more benevolent watchfulness, than human sagacity could possibly have displayed. If an obvious fitness of things—if striking institutional adaptations to man's nature and necessities—may be regarded here, as elsewhere, as proofs of intelligent design, then are we driven to the irresistible conclusion, that "the Sabbath was made for man" by his benignant Creator, and was part of the original constitution of things. For it would be irrational to suppose that these beautiful harmonies are fortuitous, or that the sum of these advantages is the result of mere accident.

It only remains for us now to draw these remarks to a close. And, in doing so, we would energetically urge upon our enlightened yokefellows the tremendous importance of being found true to themselves and to their country in the present crisis. Let them display a magnanimous firmness equal to the emergency. Let them unite and make common cause against every attempt at Sabbath spoliation and invasion. Let not the individuals of one section of the community of labour be so base and venal, as to be successfully bribed into the surrender of their own privileges, or the betrayal of the rights of their comrades. Great vigilance and wariness must be exercised; as the transference of the seventh day to mammon will not, probably, be overtly sought, but attempts will be made to bring it about gradually and stealthily—now tampering with one section, and now with another; and manifesting great care and craftiness in introducing the thin part of the wedge, which will be well edged with gold to make it work its way. Plausible pretexts will be found in abundance; for wickedness is never at a loss for specious arguments wherewith to sanctify its foulest treasons. But, by a timely persuasion of the perils by which they are menaced; by a prompt and manful decision of purpose; and by a simultaneous movement in the right direction, the crisis may be safely passed. Whilst, on the other hand, by disunion and faithlessness among themselves, by a reckless indifference to the issues of the pending contest, or by a blind and an infatuated hostility to the day, on the ground of its sanctity, such mad and suicidal conduct must lead at least to the partial overthrow of an institution conservative of peerless blessings to the working classes, and will entail upon them and their progeny an awful retribution.

Suppose the Sabbath were to be, by all people, consentaneously abolished; let the railway trains, as on other days, dart athwart the land; let the tide of commerce, unarrested, flow; let the hives of industry still swarm; let the clangor of machinery and the deafening roar of trade continue to resound; let the tramp of traffic still go on; let the greedy grasp their gains, and the slaves go groaning beneath their fetters; in short, let the contentious world proceed as at other times. And what would be the upshot of all this? Should we be the happier—the healthier—the freer—the richer? Would any one of the ends of our terrestrial existence be in any degree facilitated thereby? Would the selfishness of man, unchecked and unreproved, be less grinding or cruel? Would the oppressor be less tyrannical? Would any of the acknowledged evils of society be diminished one iota? Would the competitions, the rivalries, and the heartburnings of men be less crushing and ruinous? Alas, no! every evil under which we now writhe would be aggravated; every carnal passion would then have full swing, every undamped lust would then burn with increased intensity, health would be prematurely blasted, the nobility of man would be annihilated, and the glorious energies of his immortal spirit would be hopelessly imprisoned. Mammon and Bacchus might continue to be diligently served, but God would be unworshipped! Mankind, thus ingloriously wedded to the world, would through all their lives grovel in the dust, and never devoutly raise their foreheads to the temple of the sky!

Help, ye wearied children of labour! Help, ye Christian ministers and philanthropists! Help, ye statesmen and legislators! Help, ye patriots, whose hearts yearn for the welfare of your suffering kind! Help, that the most distant approach to such a state of things as we have just surmised may be prevented, and that the blessed advantages chartered by the Sabbath may be faithfully preserved and zealously extended.

FRONTISPIECE TO THE TORCH OF TIME.

"By this kind provision, home is still a reality."—See page 21.